EASY BANJO
SOLO FAVORITES

T0079445

CONTENTS

Banjo arrangements by Harold Streeter

Cherry Lane Music Company
Director of Publications/Project Editor: Mark Phillips

ISBN 978-1-60378-359-0

Visit our website at www.cherrylaneprint.com

AMAZING GRACE

Words by John Newton
Traditional American Melody

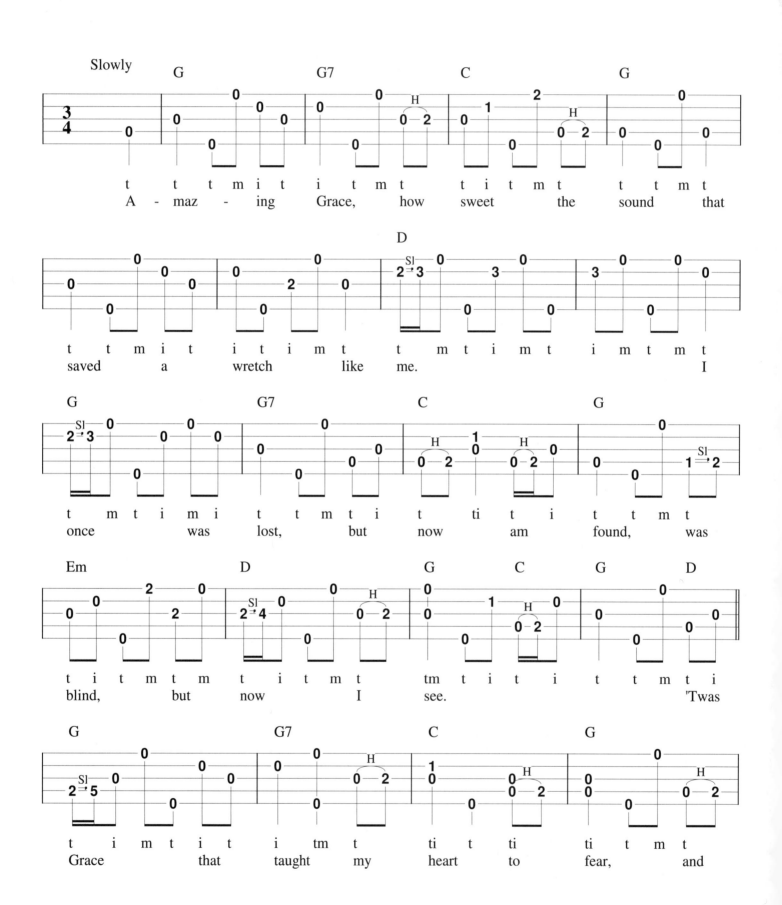

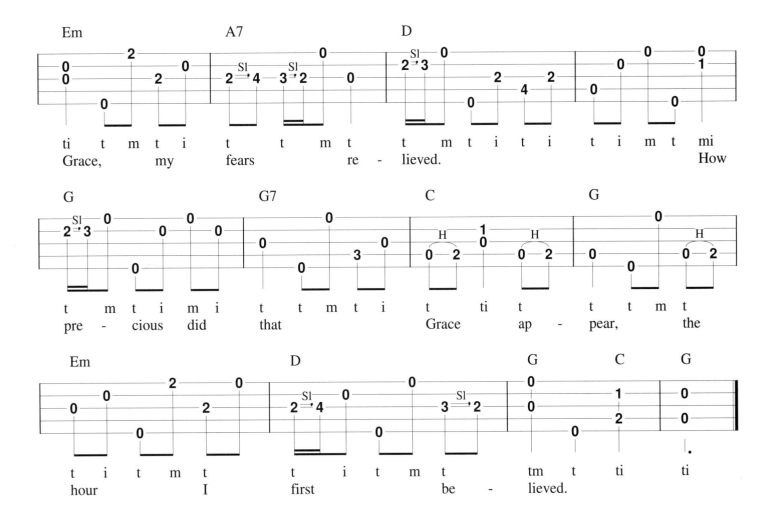

3. Through many dangers, toils and snares,
   I have already come.
   'Tis Grace that brought me safe thus far,
   And Grace will lead me home.

4. The Lord has promised good to me,
   His word my hope secures.
   He will my shield and portion be,
   As long as life endures.

5. Yea, when this flesh and heart shall fail,
   And mortal life shall cease,
   I shall possess within the veil,
   A life of joy and peace.

6. When we've been here ten thousand years,
   Bright shining as the sun,
   We've no less days to sing God's praise,
   Than when we've first begun.

BAD MOON RISING

Words and Music by
John Fogerty

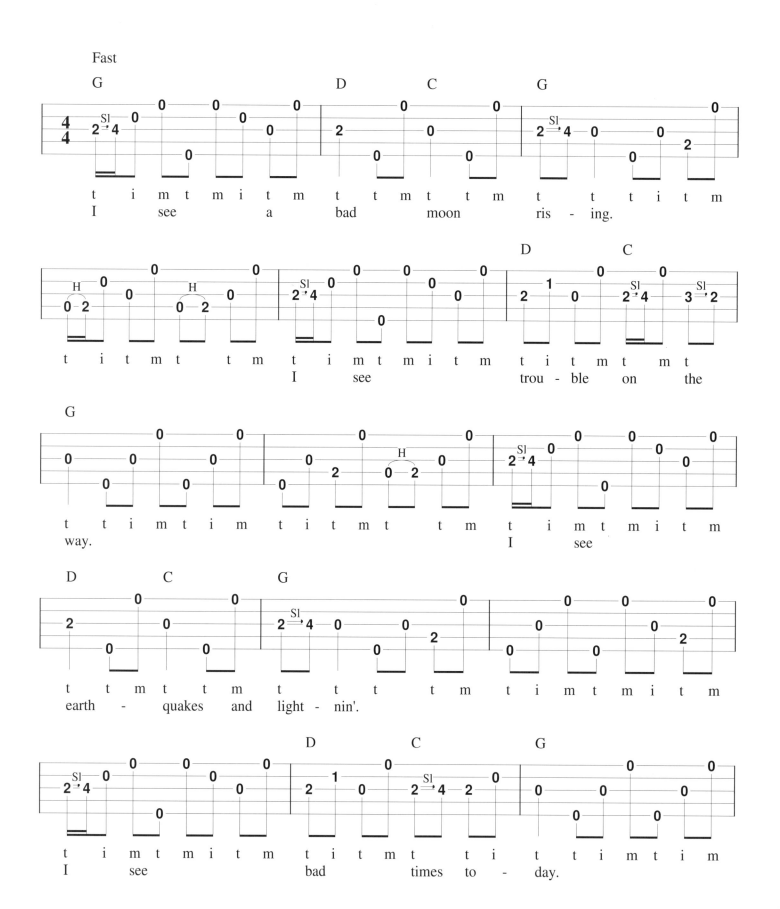

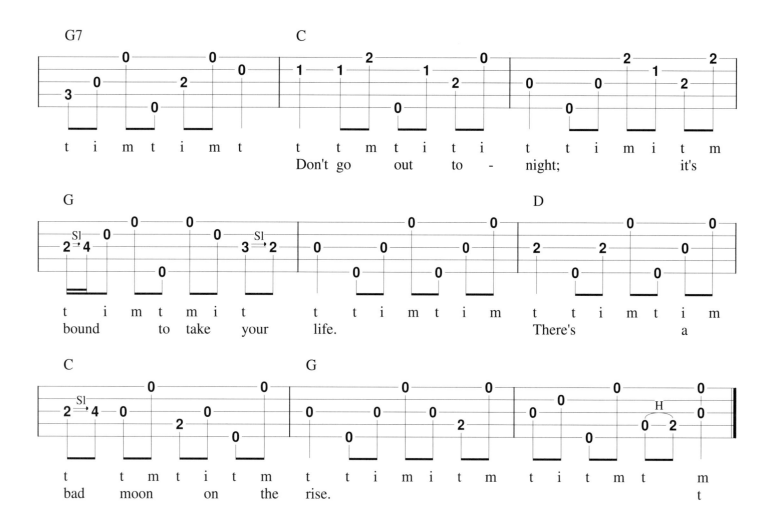

2. I hear hurricanes a-blowing.
   I know the end is coming soon.
   I fear rivers over flowing.
   I hear the voice of rage and ruin.

   Don't go out tonight, etc.

3. Hope you got your things together,
   Hope you are quite prepared to die.
   Looks like we're in for nasty weather.
   One eye is taken for an eye.

   Don't go out tonight, etc.

BALLAD OF JED CLAMPETT

from the Television Series THE BEVERLY HILLBILLIES

Words and Music by
Paul Henning

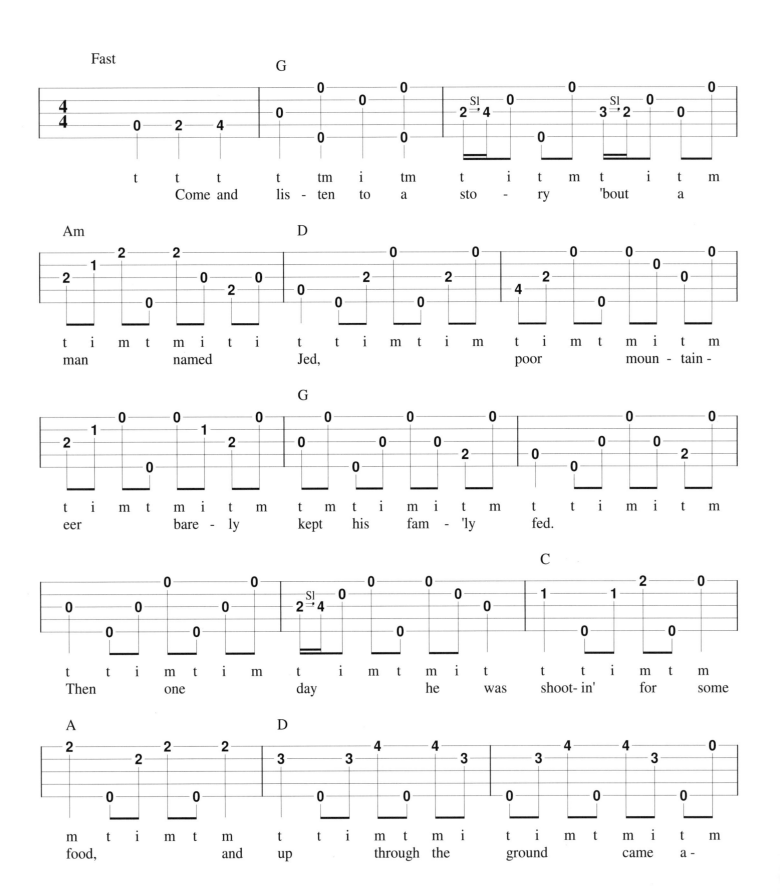

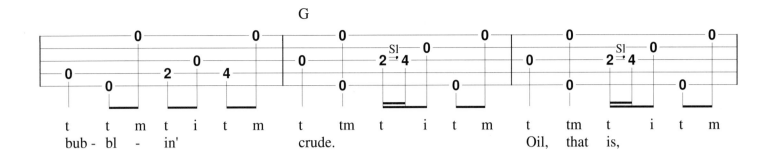

bub - bl - in' crude. Oil, that is,

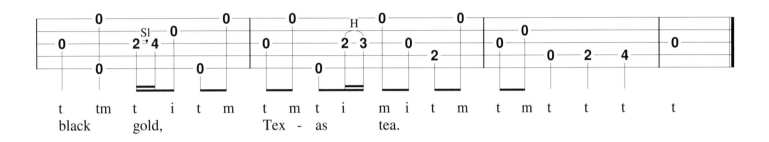

black gold, Tex - as tea.

2. Well, the first thing you know old Jed's a millionaire.
   Kin folk said, "Jed move away from there."
   Said California is the place you oughta be,
   So they loaded up the truck and they moved to Beverly,
   Hills, that is, swimming pools, movie stars.

3. Well, now it's time to say goodbye to Jed and all his kin.
   They would like to thank you folks for kindly dropping in.
   You're all invited back again to this locality
   To have a heaping helping of their hospitality.
   Beverly Hillbillies, that's what they call 'em now.
   Nice folks, y'all come back now, ya hear?

BLACKBERRY BLOSSOM

Traditional

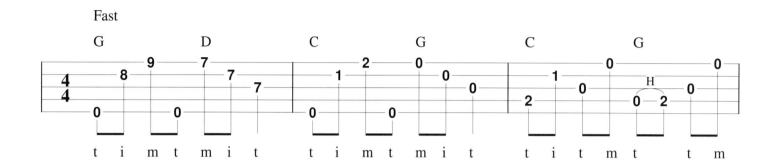

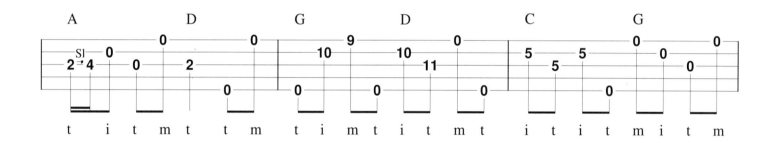

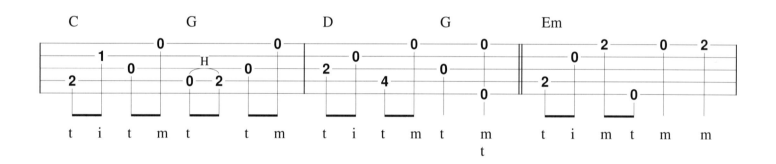

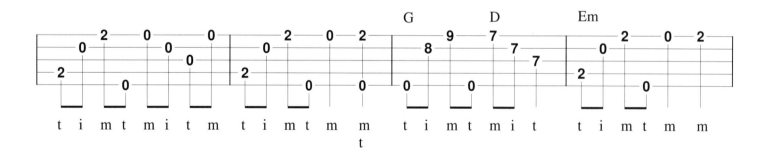

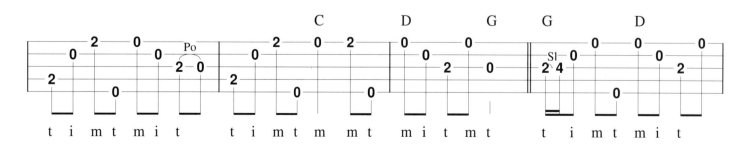

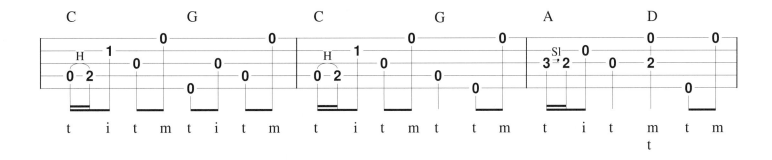

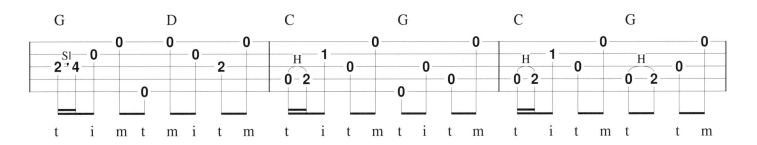

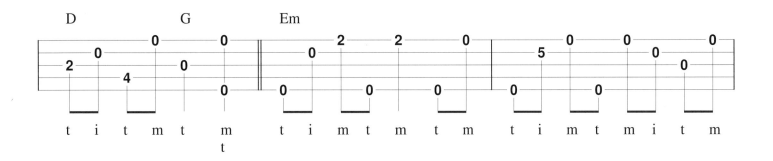

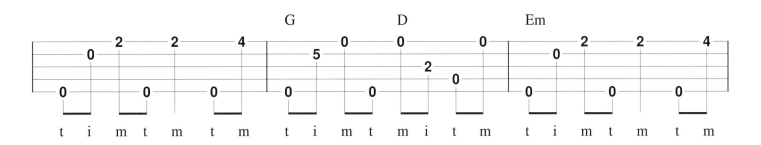

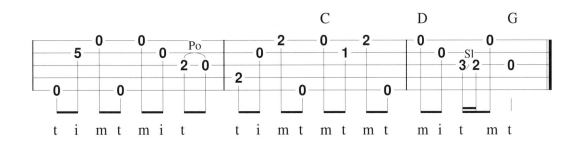

BLOWIN' IN THE WIND

Words and Music by
Bob Dylan

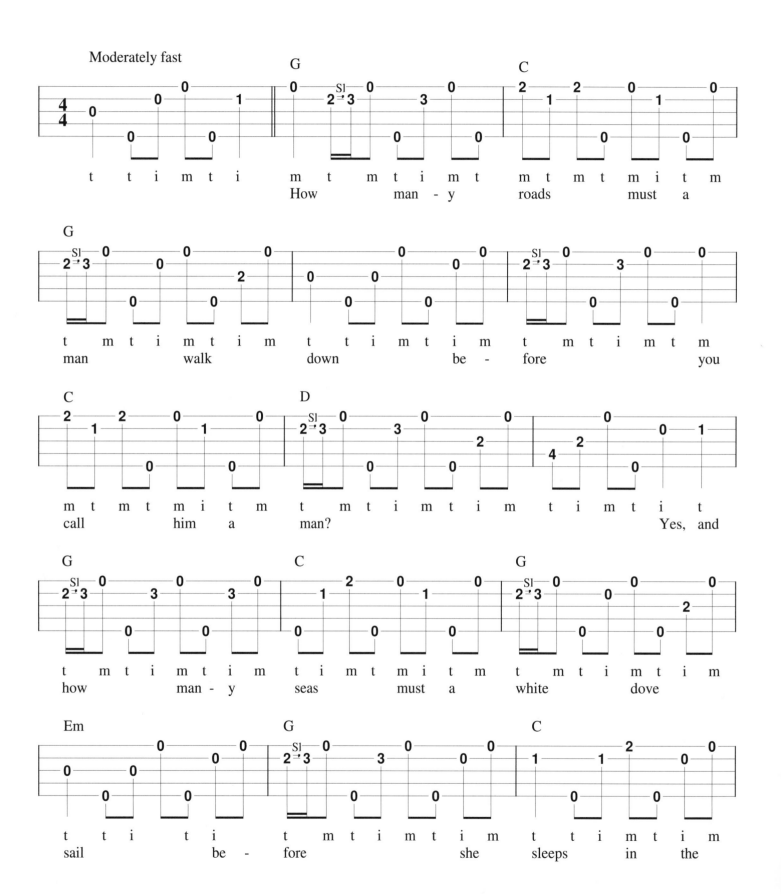

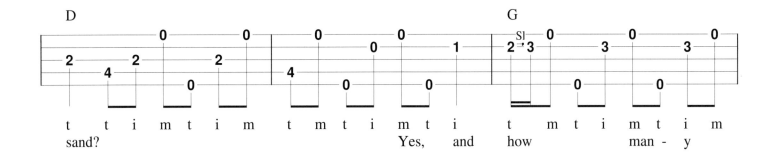

sand?   Yes,   and   how   man - y

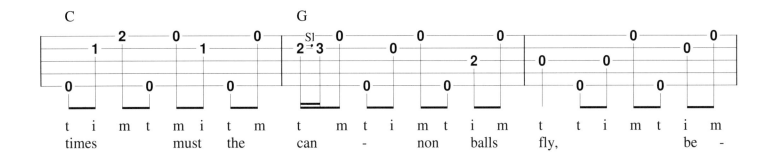

times   must the   can -   non   balls   fly,   be -

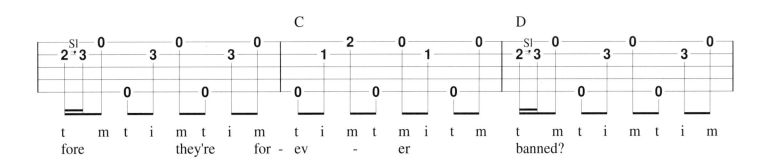

fore   they're   for - ev   -   er   banned?

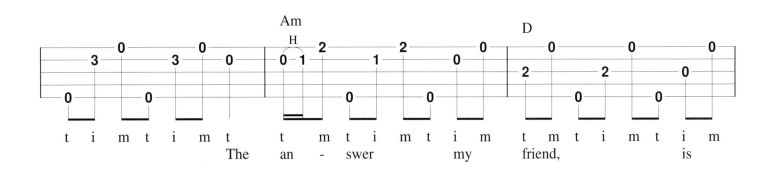

The   an - swer   my   friend,   is

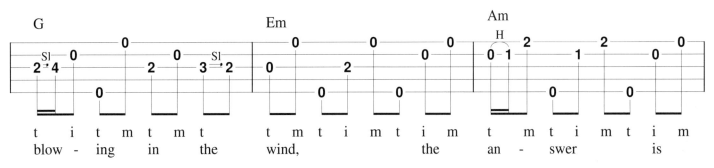

blow - ing   in   the   wind,   the   an - swer   is

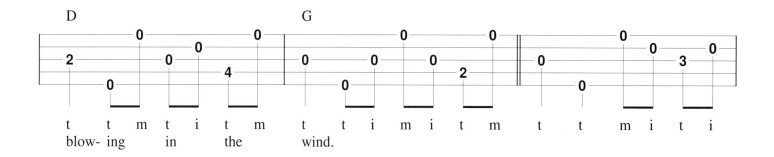

t t m t i t m t t i m i t m t t m i t i
blow- ing in the wind.

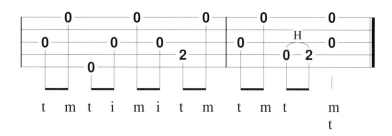

t m t i m i t m t m t m
t

2. How many times must a man look up
   Before he can see the sky?
   Yes, and how many ears must one man have
   Before he can hear people cry?
   Yes, and how many deaths will it take till he knows
   That too many people have died?
   The answer, my friend, is blowin' in the wind,
   The answer is blowin' in the wind.

3. How many years can a mountain exist
   Before it's washed to the sea?
   Yes, and how many years can some people exist
   Before they're allowed to be free?
   Yes, and how many times can a man turn his head
   Pretending he just doesn't see?
   The answer, my friend, is blowin' in the wind,
   The answer is blowin' in the wind.

CAT'S IN THE CRADLE

Words and Music by
Harry Chapin and Sandy Chapin

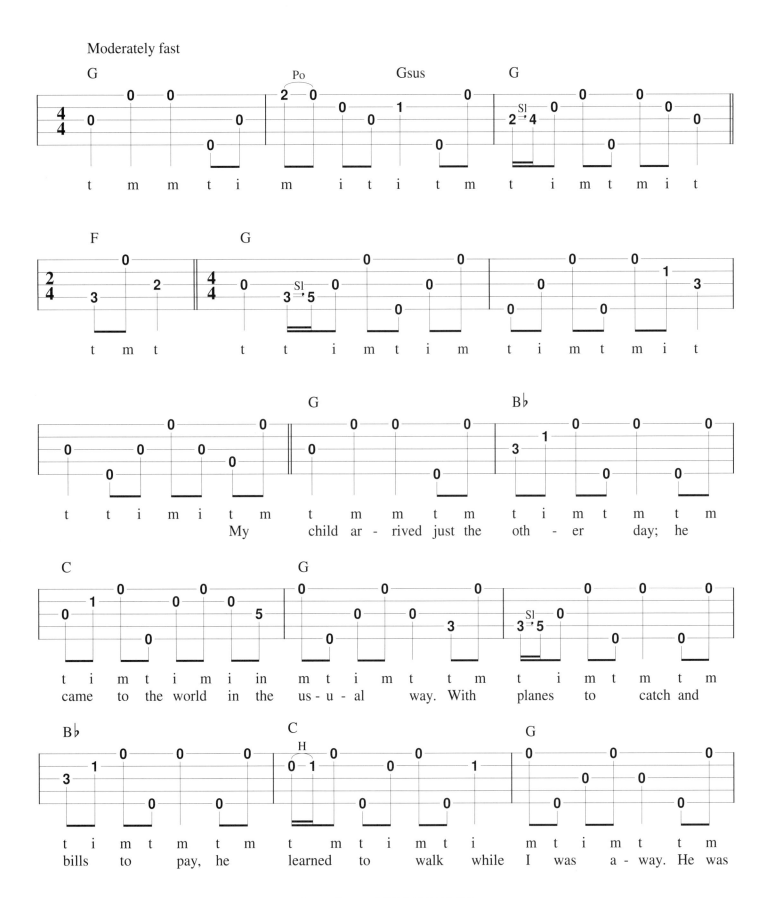

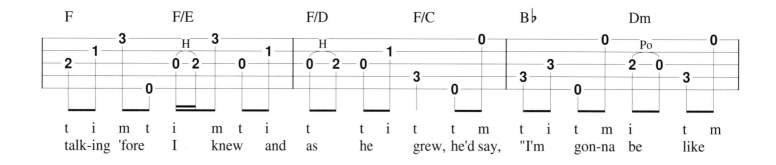

talk-ing 'fore I knew and as he grew, he'd say, "I'm gon-na be like

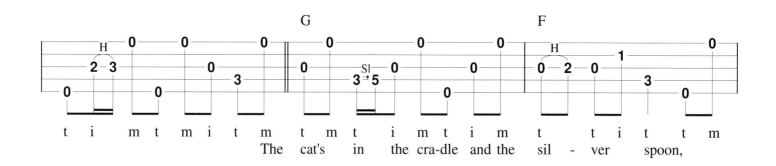

you, Dad. I'm gon-na be like you."

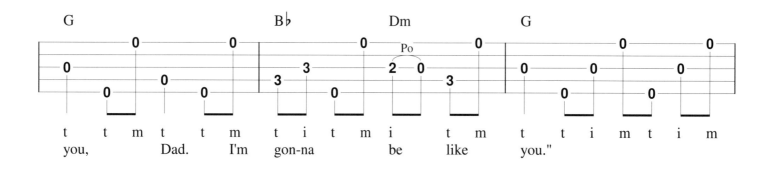

The cat's in the cra-dle and the sil - ver spoon,

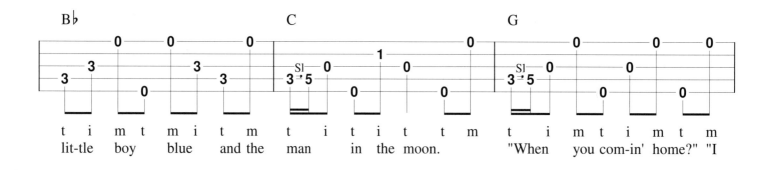

lit-tle boy blue and the man in the moon. "When you com-in' home?" "I

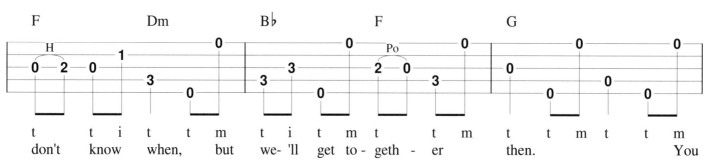

don't know when, but we-'ll get to - geth - er then. You

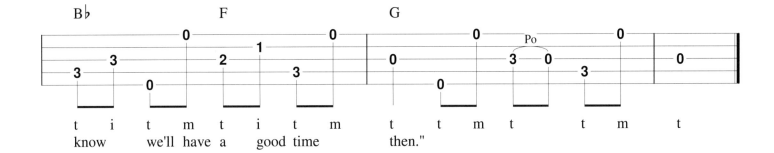

2. My son turned ten just the other day; he said, "Thanks for the ball, Dad; come on let's play.
Can you teach me to throw?" I said, "Not today, I got a lot to do." He said, "Thats okay."
And then he walked away but his smile never dimmed, and said, "I'm gonna be like him, yeah,
You know I'm going to be like him."

And the cat's in the cradle and the silver spoon, little boy blue and the man in the moon.
"When you comin' home, Dad?" "I dont know when, but we'll get together then.
You know we'll have a good time then."

3. Well, he came from college just the other day, so much like a man I just had to say,
"Son, I'm proud of you, can you sit for a while?" He shook his head, and he said with a smile;
"What I'd really like, Dad, is to borrow the car keys; see you later, can I have them please?"

And the cat's in the cradle and the silver spoon, little boy blue and the man in the moon.
"When you comin' home, Son?" "I dont know when, but we'll get together then, Dad,
You know we'll have a good time then."

4. I've long since retired, my son's moved away; I called him up just the other day.
I said, "I'd like to see you if you don't mind." He said, "I'd love to, Dad, if I could find the time.
You see, my new job's a hassle, and the kids have the flu, but it's sure nice talking to you, Dad.
It's been sure nice talking to you."

And as I hung up the phone it occurred to me, he'd grown up just like me.
My boy was just like me.

And the cat's in the cradle and the silver spoon, little boy blue and the man in the moon.
"When you comin' home, Son?" "I dont know when, but we'll get together then, Dad.
We're gonna have a good time then."

THE BOXER

Words and Music by
Paul Simon

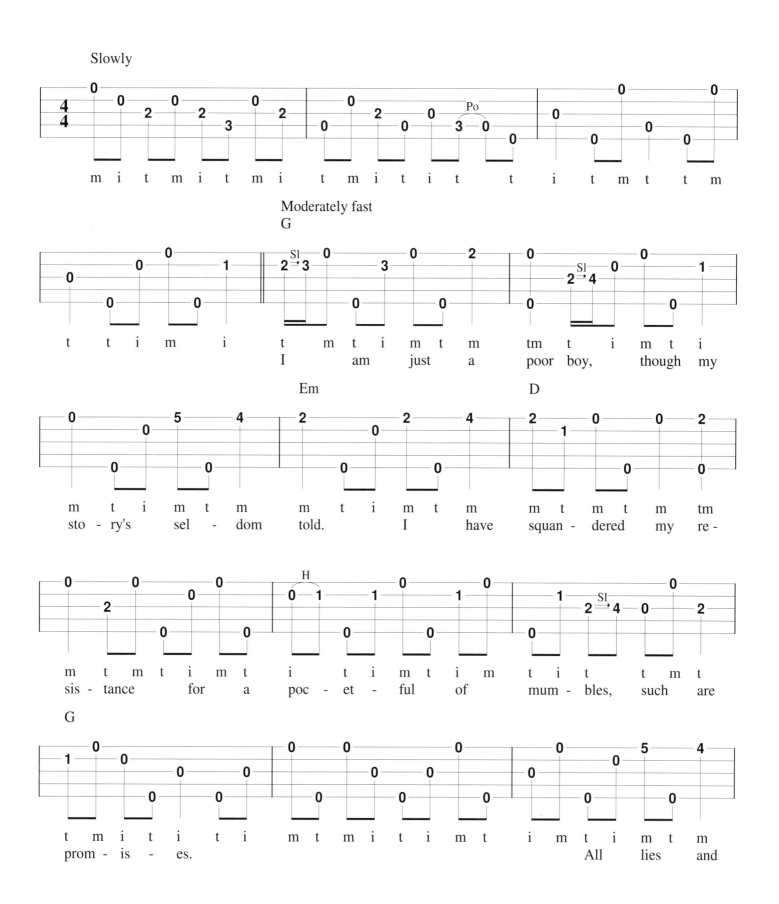

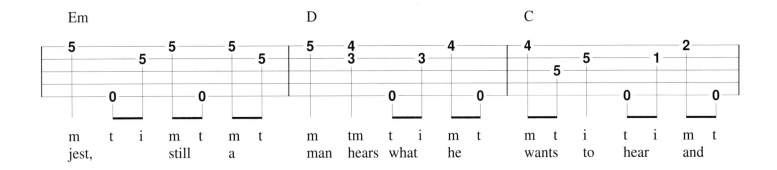

jest, still a man hears what he wants to hear and

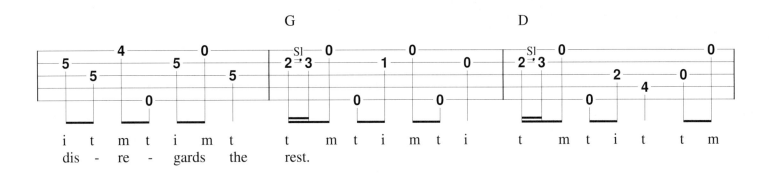

dis - re - gards the rest.

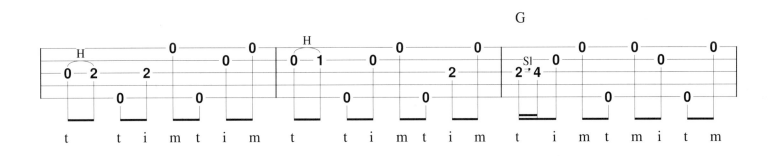

When I

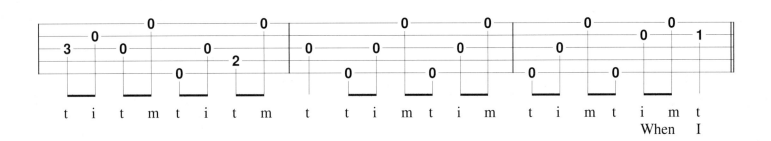

left my home and fam - i - ly, I was no more than a

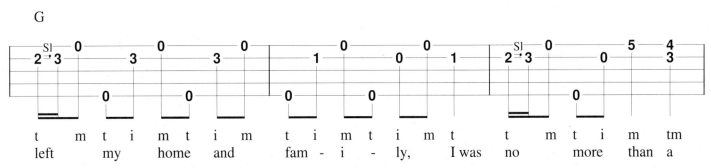

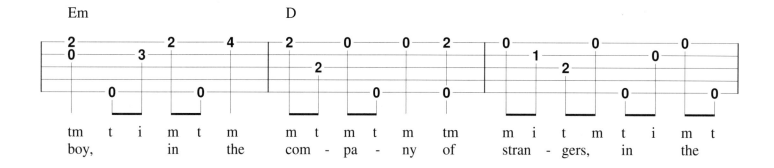

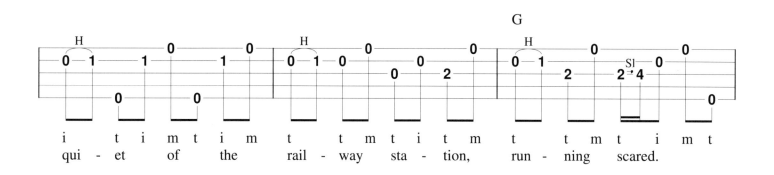

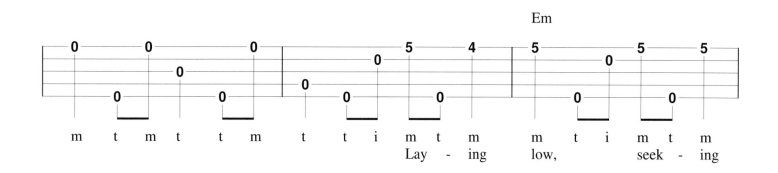

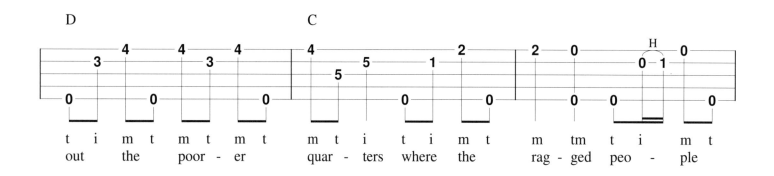

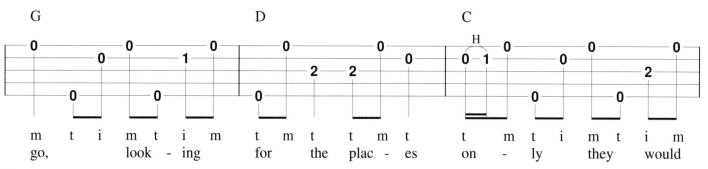

G

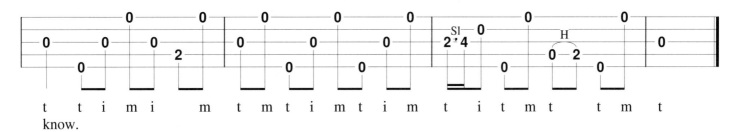

| t | t | i | m | i | | m | t | m | t | i | m | t | i | m | t | i | t | m | t | | t | m | t |

know.

3. Asking only workman's wages I come looking for a job,
   But I get no offers, just a come-on from the whores on Seventh Avenue.
   I do declare, there were times when I was so lonesome,
   I took some comfort there.

4. Then I'm laying out my winter clothes, and wishing I was gone,
   Going home where the New York City winters aren't bleeding me,
   Leading me, going home.

5. In the clearing stands a boxer, a fighter by his trade,
   And he carries the reminders of every glove that laid him down
   And cut him till he cried out in his anger and his shame,
   "I am leaving, I am leaving." But the fighter still remains.

CITY OF NEW ORLEANS

Words and Music by
Steve Goodman

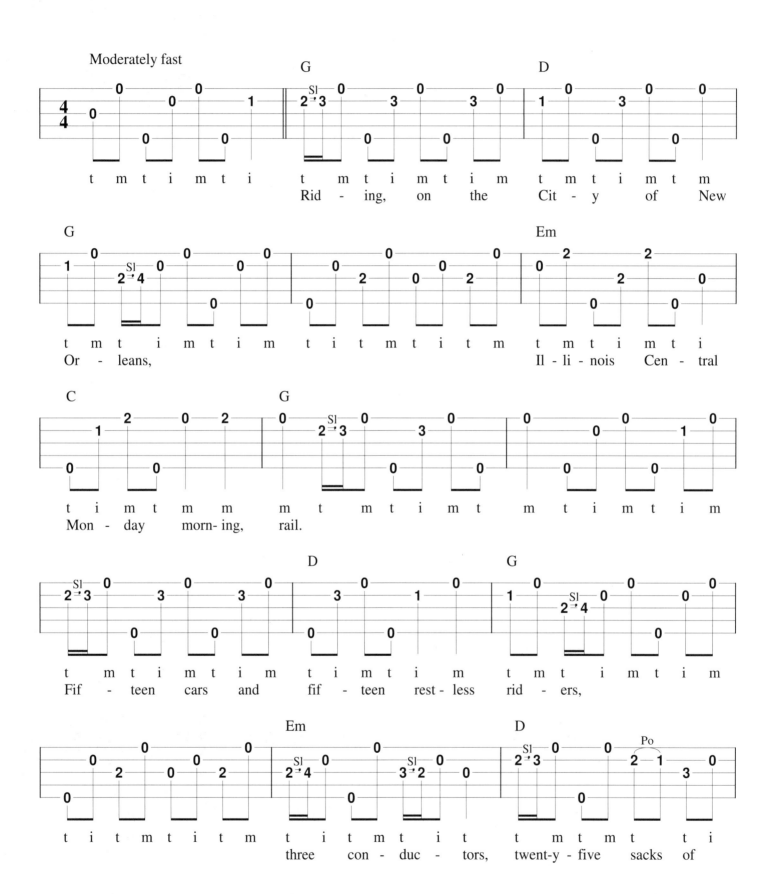

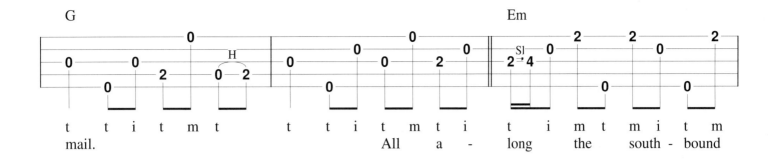

t   t   i   t   m   t   t   t   i   t   m   i   t   i   m   t   m   i   t   m

mail.   All   a - long   the   south - bound

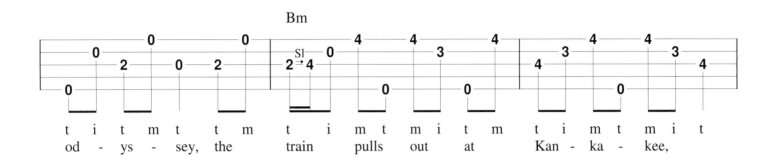

t   i   t   m   t   t   m   t   i   m   t   m   i   t   m   t   i   m   t   m   i   t

od - ys - sey, the   train   pulls   out   at   Kan - ka - kee,

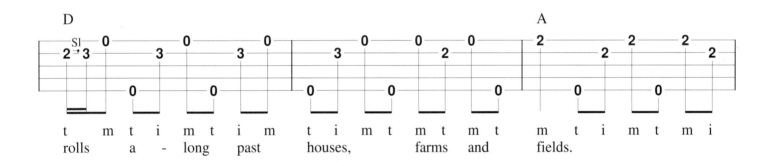

t   m   t   i   m   t   i   m   t   i   m   t   m   t   m   m   t   i   m   t   m   i

rolls   a - long   past   houses,   farms   and   fields.

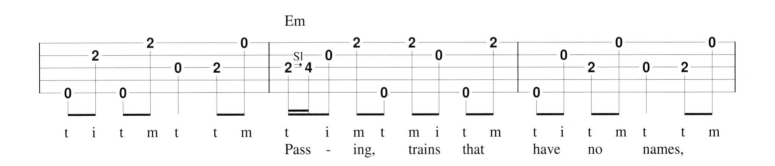

t   i   t   m   t   t   m   t   i   m   t   m   i   t   m   t   i   t   m   t   t   m

Pass - ing, trains   that   have   no   names,

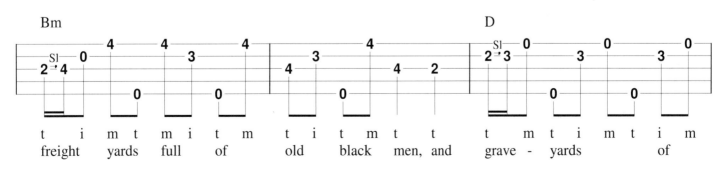

t   i   m   t   m   i   t   m   t   i   t   m   t   t   t   m   t   i   m   t   i   m

freight   yards   full   of   old   black   men, and   grave - yards   of

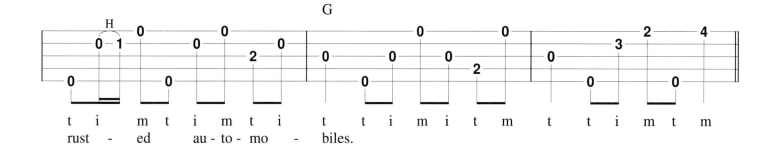

rust - ed   au - to - mo - biles.

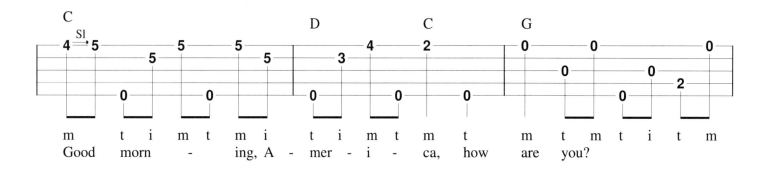

Good morn - ing, A - mer - i - ca, how   are   you?

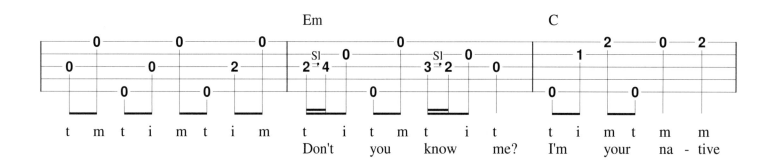

Don't   you   know   me?   I'm   your   na - tive

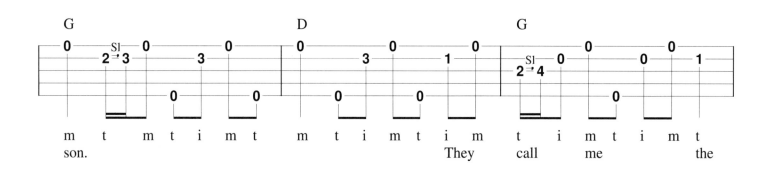

son.   They   call   me   the

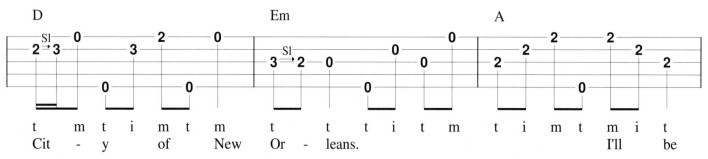

Cit - y   of   New   Or - leans.   I'll   be

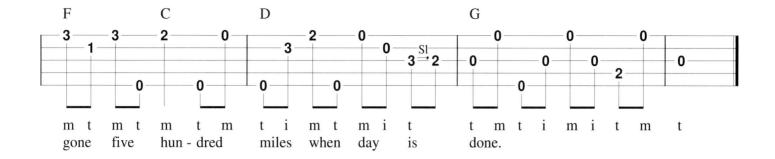

m t   m t   m   t   m   t   i   m t   m   i   t   t   m   t   i   m   i   t   m   t

gone   five   hun - dred   miles when day   is   done.

2. Dealin' card games with the old men in the club car,
   Penny a point, no one's keeping score.
   Pass the paper bag that holds the bottle,
   Feel the wheels rumbling 'neath the floor.

   And the sons of pullman porters, and the sons of engineers
   Ride their fathers' magic carpets made of steel.
   Mothers with their babes asleep are rockin' to the gentle beat,
   And the rhythm of the rails is all they feel.

   Good morning, America, how are you?
   Don't you know me? I'm your native son.
   I'm the train they call the City of New Orleans.
   I'll be gone five hundred miles when the day is done.

3. Nighttime on the City of New Orleans,
   Changing cars in Memphis, Tennessee.
   Halfway home, we'll be there by morning,
   Through the Mississippi darkness rolling down to the sea.

   And all the towns and people seem to fade into a bad dream,
   And the steel rails still ain't heard the news.
   The conductor sings his song again, the passengers will please refrain.
   This train's got the disappearing railroad blues.

   Good night, America, how are you?
   Don't you know me? I'm your native son.
   I'm the train they call the City of New Orleans.
   I'll be gone five hundred miles when the day is done.

COLD HEARTED

Words and Music by
Zac Brown and Nic Cowan

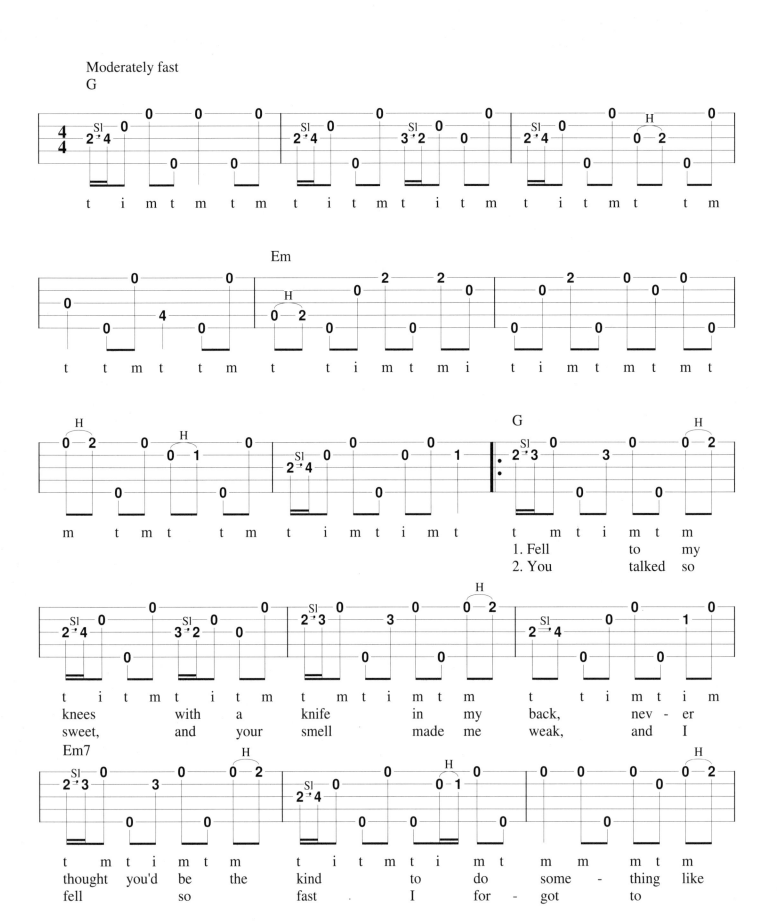

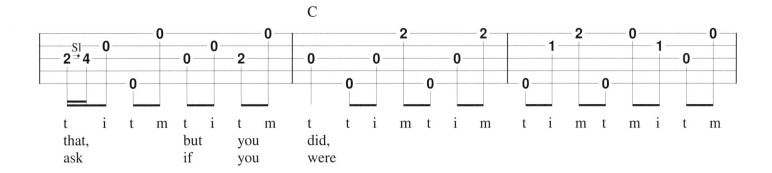

that, but you did,
ask if you were

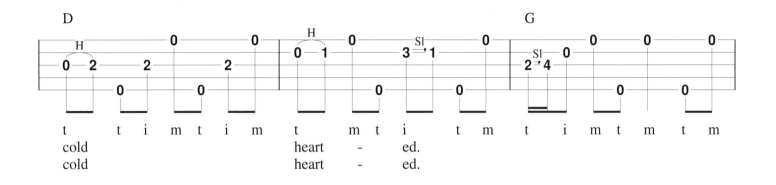

cold heart - ed.
cold heart - ed.

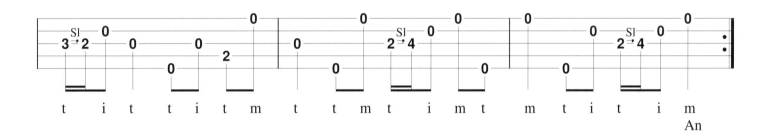

An

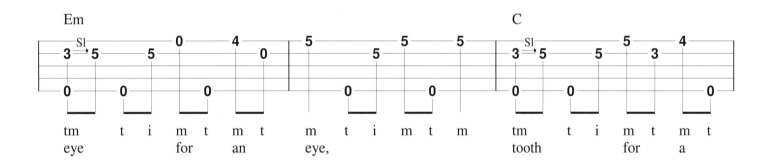

eye for an eye, tooth for a

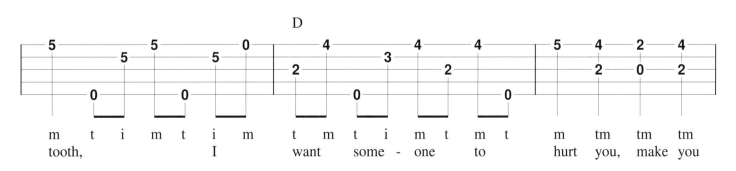

tooth, I want some - one to hurt you, make you

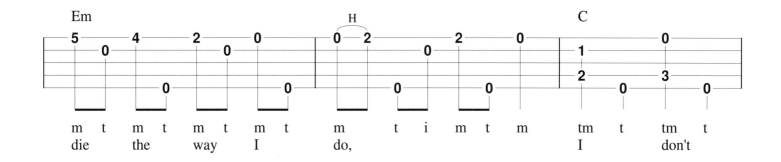

die the way I do,   I don't

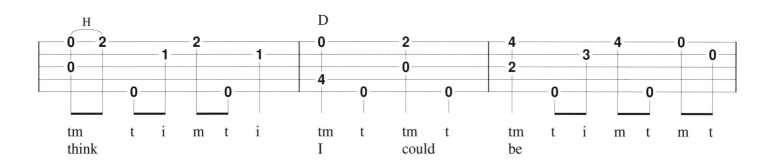

think I could be

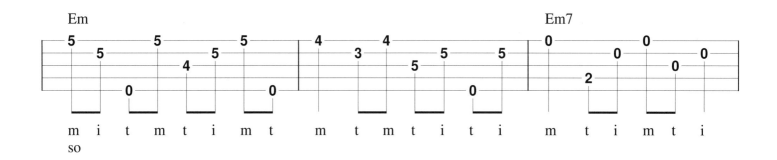

so

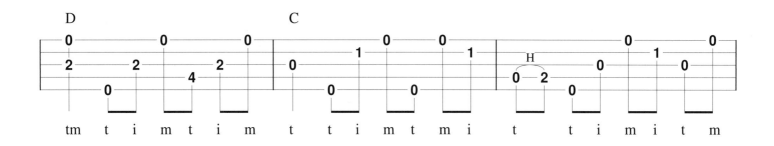

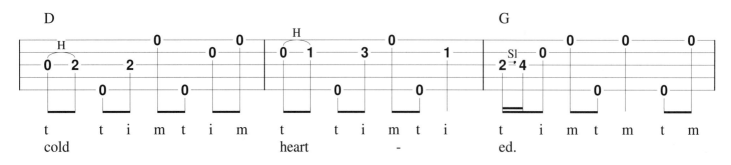

cold   heart - ed.

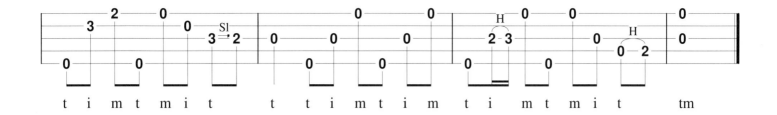

3. Pretty little words covered your dark and crooked heart.
   With a forked tongue I fell in love, then I fell apart.
   You are so cold hearted.

   Chorus

   An eye for an eye, tooth for a tooth,
   I want someone to hurt you, make you die the way I do.
   I don't think that I could be so cold hearted.

   Repeat Chorus

CRIPPLE CREEK

American Fiddle Tune

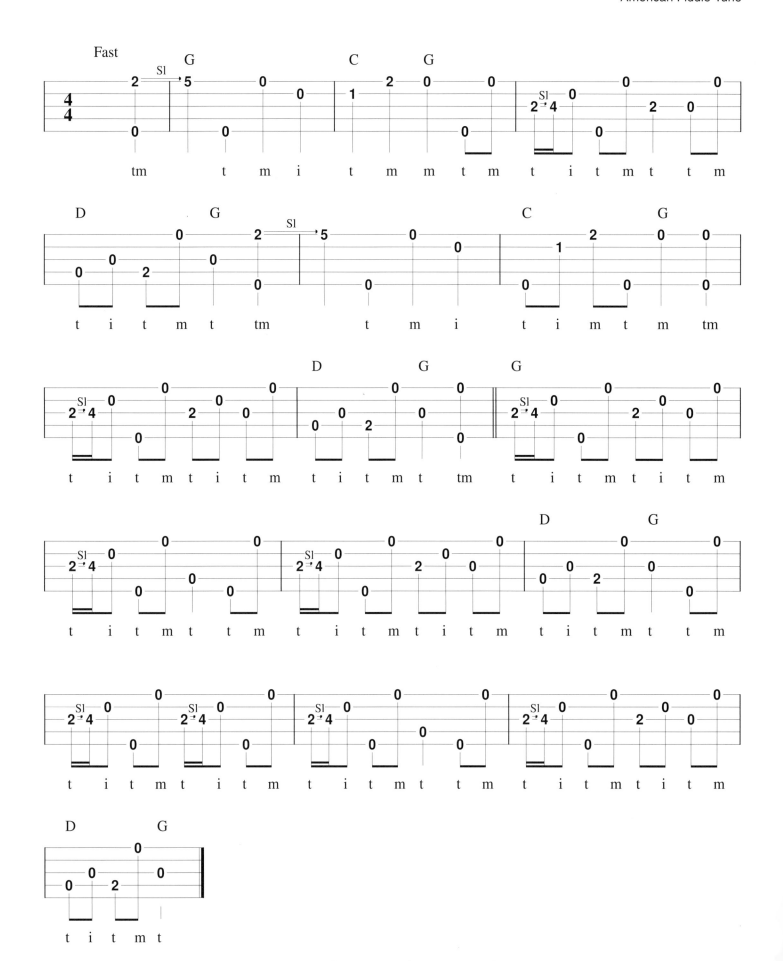

DANNY'S SONG

Words and Music by
Kenny Loggins

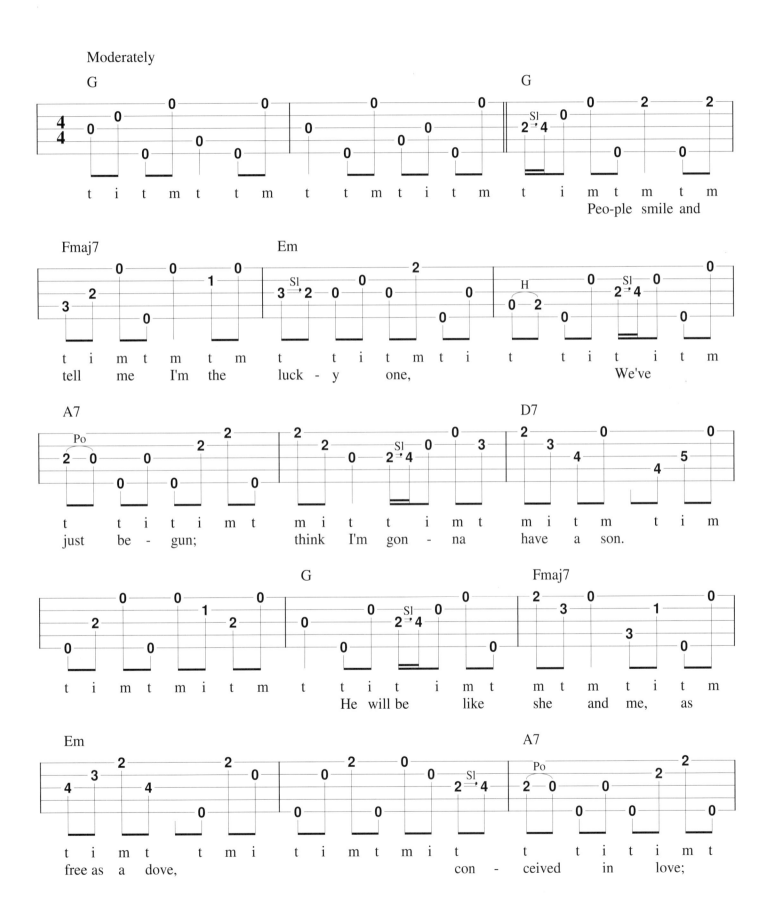

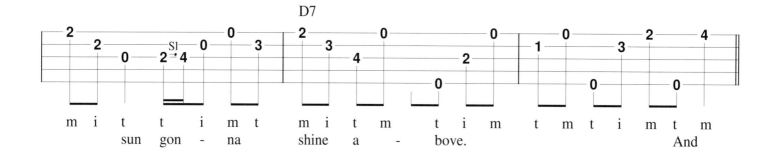

m i t t i m t
sun gon - na

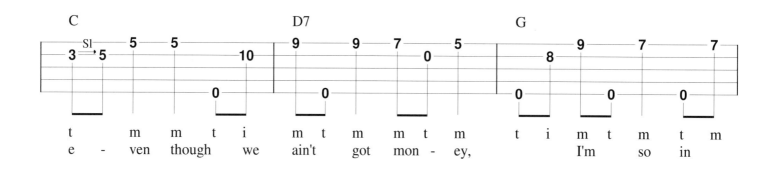

m i t m t i m t m t i m t m
shine a - bove. And

C
t m m t i
e - ven though we

D7
m t m m t m
ain't got mon - ey,

G
t i m t m t m
I'm so in

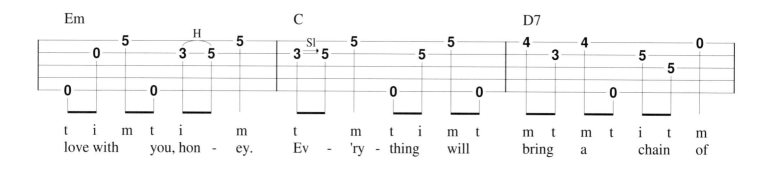

Em
t i m t i m
love with you, hon - ey.

C
t m t i m t
Ev - 'ry - thing will

D7
m t m t i t m
bring a chain of

G
t i m t m m
love.

Em
tm t i m t m i
And in the morn- ing

C
t i m t m t i
And in the morn- ing

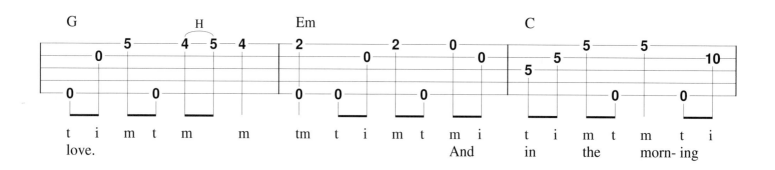

D7
m t m m t m
when I rise, you

G
t i m t m t m
bring a tear of

Fmaj7
i m i tm t m
joy to my eyes and

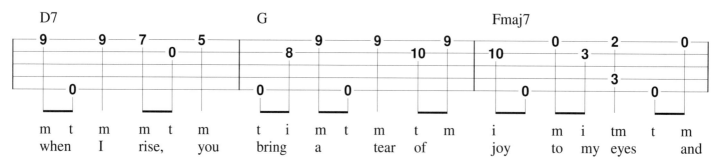

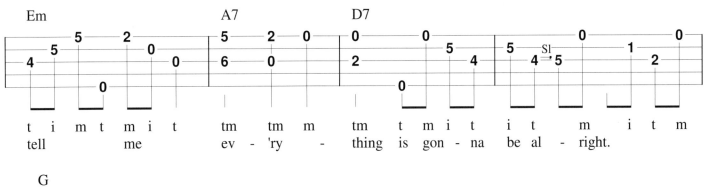

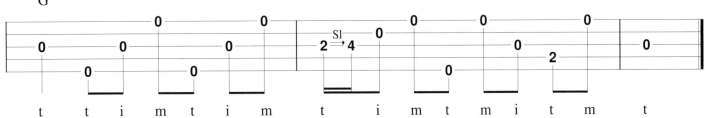

2. Seems as though a month ago I was Beta Chi.
   Never got high; oh, I was a sorry guy.
   And now I smile and face the girl that shares my name.
   Now I'm through with the game; this boy will never be the same.

   Chorus

   And even though we ain't got money, I'm so in love with you, honey,
   And everything will bring a chain of love.
   And in the morning, when I rise, you bring a tear of joy to my eyes
   And tell me everything is gonna be alright.

3. Pisces, Virgo rising is a very good sign,
   Strong and kind, and the little boy is mine.
   Now I see a family where the once was none.
   Now we've just begun; yeah, we're gonna fly to the sun.

   Repeat Chorus

4. Love the girl who holds the world in a paper cup.
   Drink it up, love her, and she'll bring you luck.
   And if you find she helps your mind, better take her home.
   Don't you live alone; try to earn what lovers own.

   Repeat Chorus

DON'T THINK TWICE, IT'S ALL RIGHT

Words and Music by
Bob Dylan

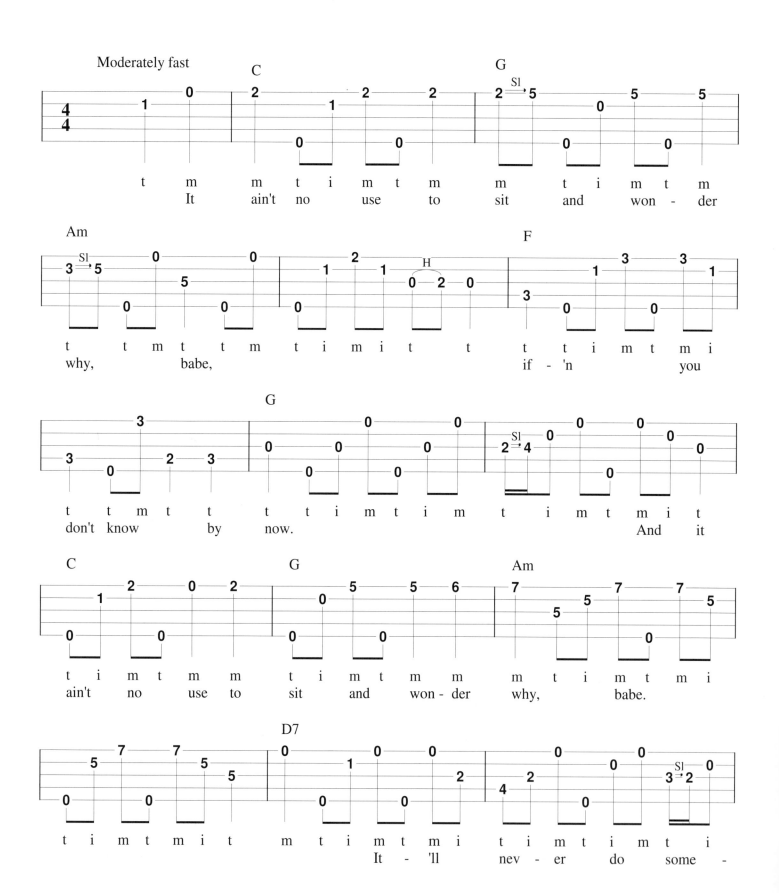

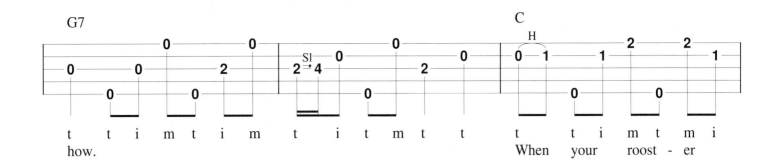

t t i m t i m
how.

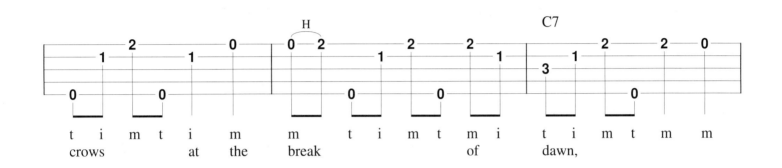

t t i m t t t t i m t m i
When your roost - er

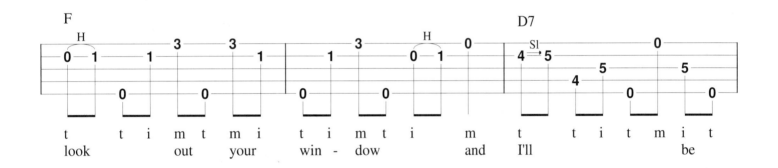

t i m t i m m t i m t m i t i m t m m
crows at the break of dawn,

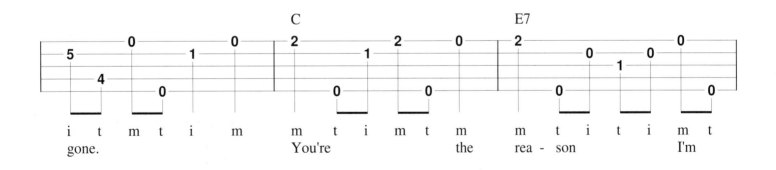

t t i m t m i t i m t m i t t i t m i t
look out your win - dow and I'll be

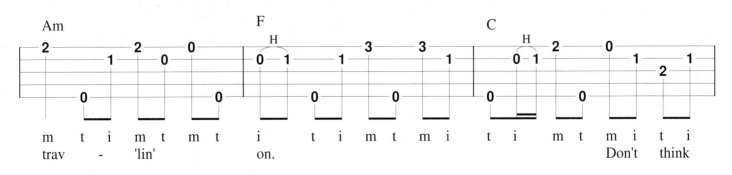

5 i t m t i m m t i m t m m t i t i m t
gone. You're the rea - son I'm

m t i m t m t i m t m i t i m t m i t i
trav - 'lin' on. Don't think

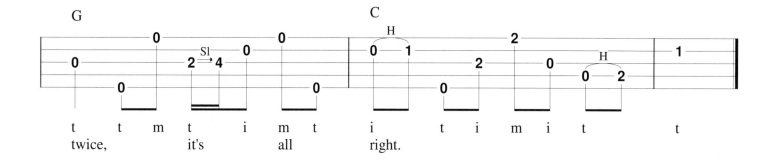

2. It ain't no use in turnin' on your light, babe;
   That light I never knowed.
   And it ain't no use in turnin' on your light, babe;
   I'm on the dark side of the road.
   But I wish there was somethin' you would do or say
   To try and make me change my mind and stay.
   We never did too much talkin' anyway,
   So don't think twice, it's all right.

3. It ain't no use in callin' out my name, gal,
   Like you never done before.
   It ain't no use in callin' out my name, gal;
   I can't hear you any more.
   I'm a-thinkin' and a-wond'rin', walkin' down the road,
   I once loved a woman, a child I'm told.
   I gave her my heart but she wanted my soul,
   But don't think twice, it's all right.

4. So long, honey babe,
   Where I'm bound, I can't tell.
   But goodbye's too good a word, babe,
   So I'll just say fare thee well.
   I ain't sayin' you treated me unkind.
   You could have done better, but I don't mind.
   You just kinda wasted my precious time,
   But don't think twice, it's all right.

DUELIN' BANJOS

By Arthur Smith

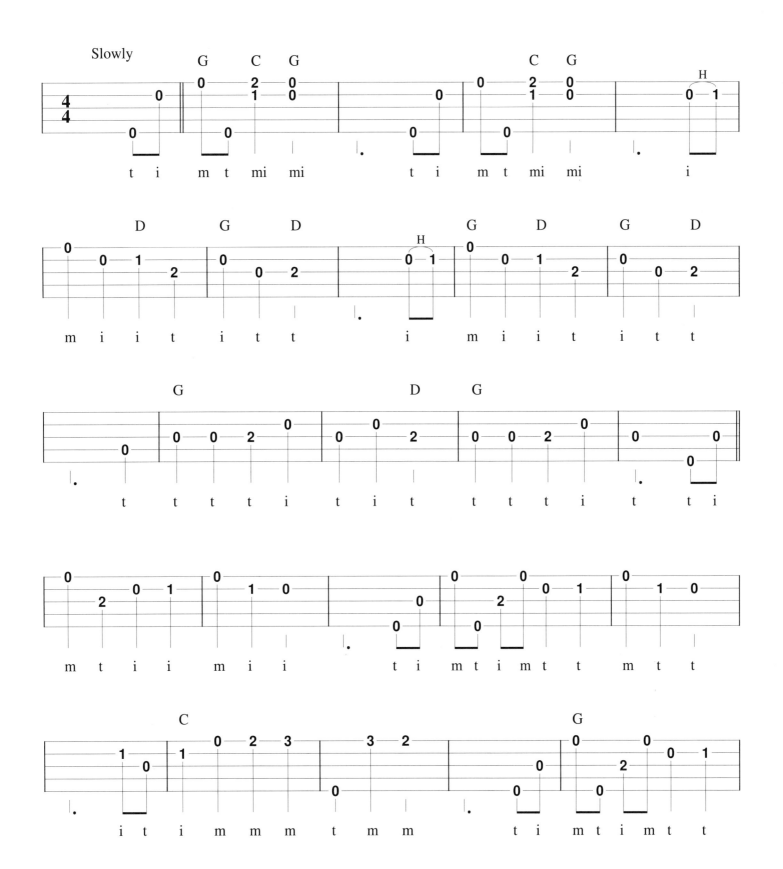

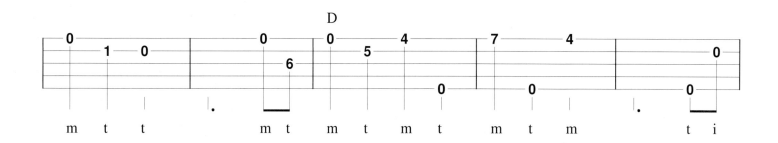

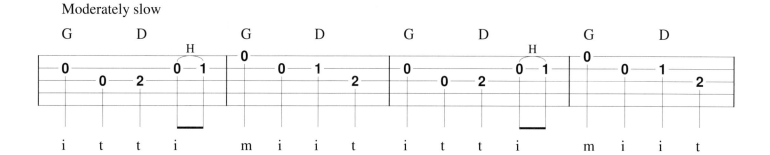

Moderately slow

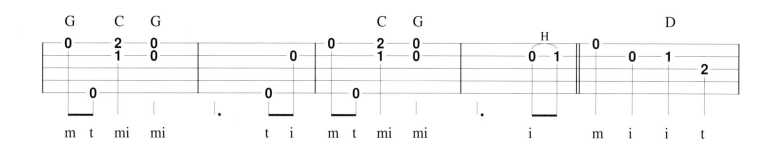

Moderately fast

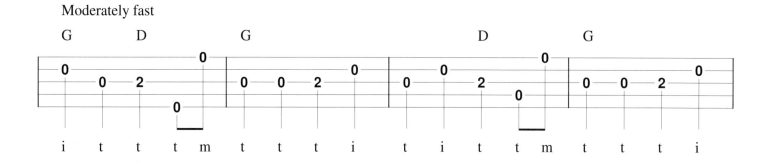

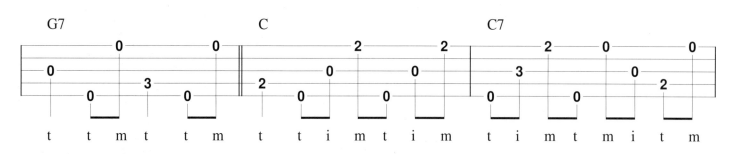

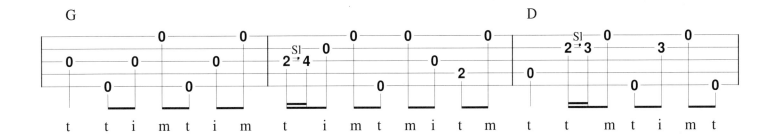

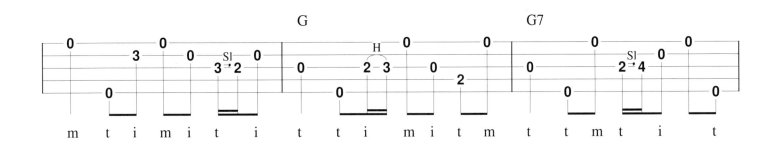

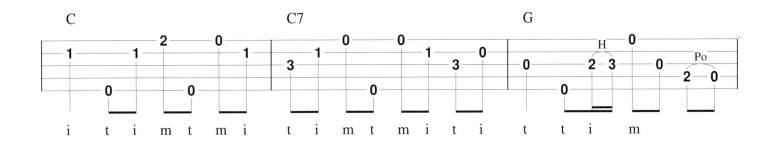

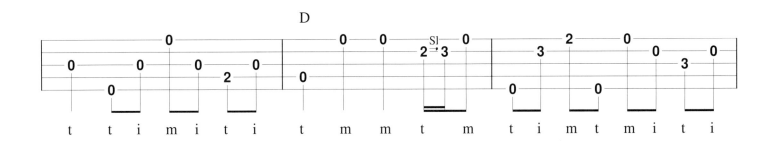

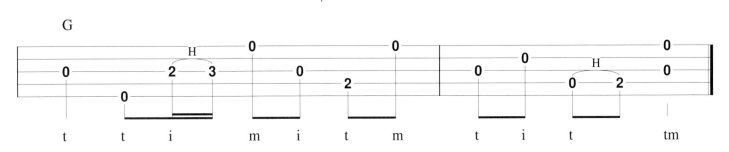

DOWN IN THE WILLOW GARDEN

Traditional

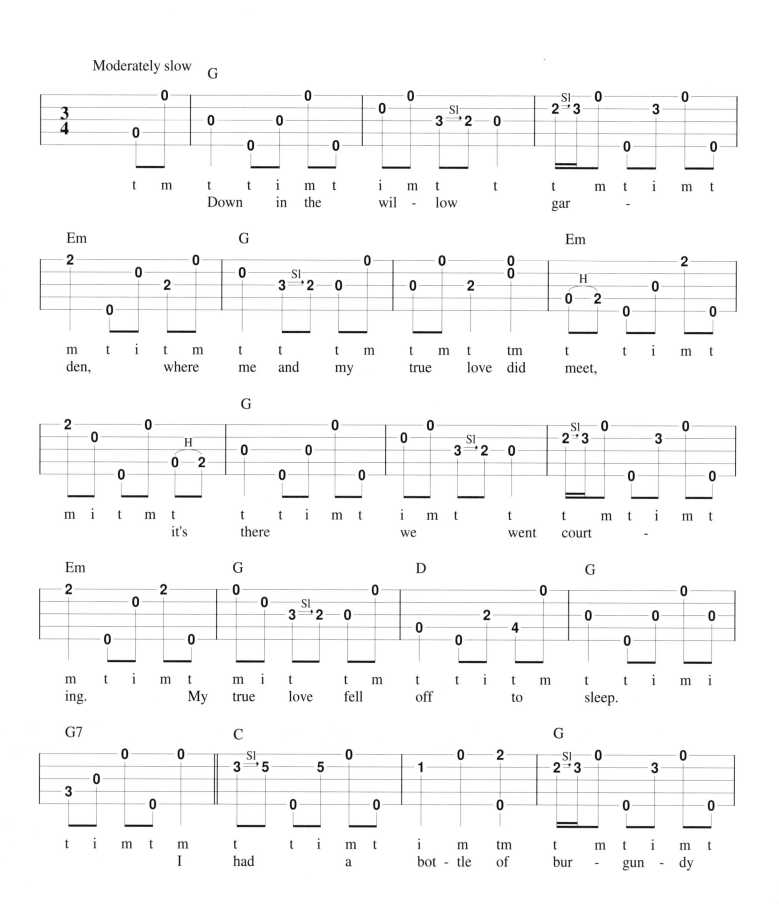

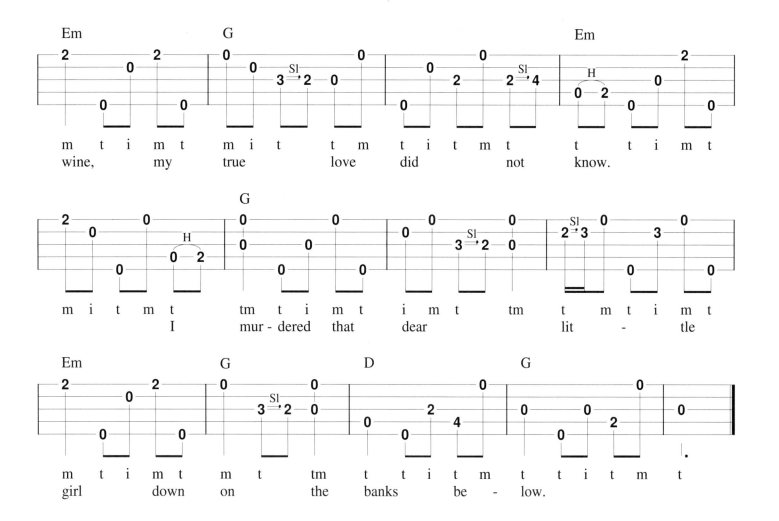

2. I drew my saber through her;
   It was a bloody knife.
   I threw her into the river;
   It was an awful sight.

   My father often told me
   That money would set me free
   If I'd but murder that dear little girl
   Whose name was Rose Connelly.

3. Now he stands at his cabin door,
   Wiping his tear dimmed eye,
   Gazing on his own dear son,
   Upon the scaffold high.

   My race is run beneath the sun;
   The devil is waiting for me.
   For I did murder that dear little girl
   Whose name was Rose Connelly.

FIRE ON THE MOUNTAIN

Words and Music by
George McCorkle

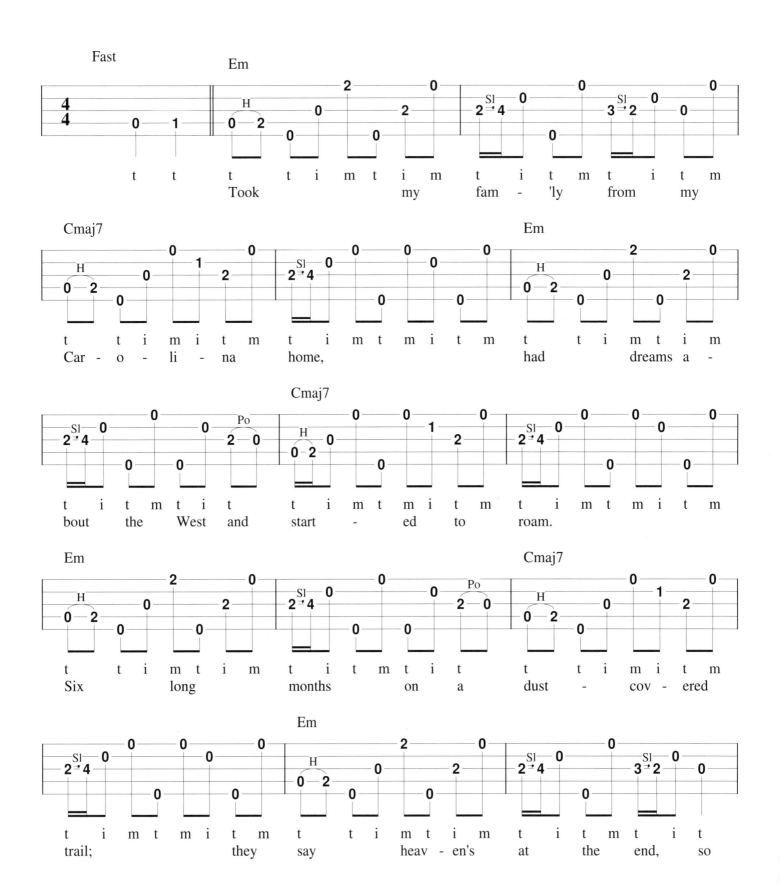

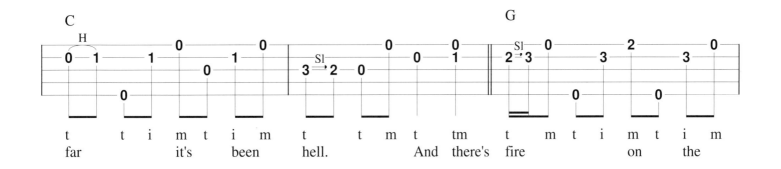

far   it's   been   hell.   And   there's   fire   on   the

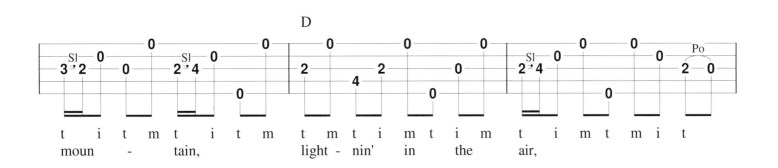

moun -   tain,   light - nin'   in   the   air,

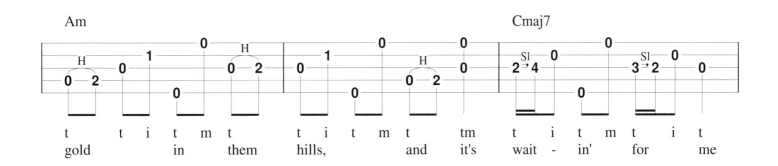

gold   in   them hills,   and   it's   wait - in'   for   me

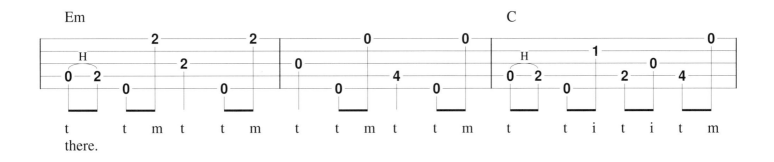

there.

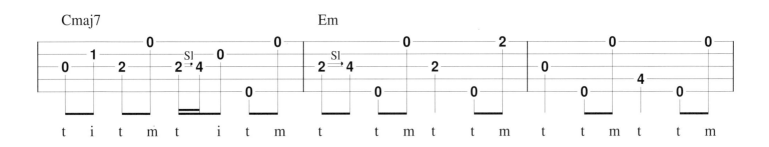

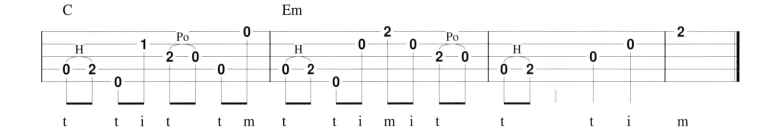

2. We were diggin' and siftin' from five to five,
   Sellin' everything we found just to stay alive.
   Gold flowed free like the whiskey in the bars.
   Sinnin' was the big thing, Lord, and Satan was his star.

   And there's fire on the mountain, lightnin' in the air,
   Gold in them hills, and it's waitin' for me there.

3. Dance hall girls were the evenin' treat;
   Empty cartridges and blood lined the gutters of the street.
   Men were shot down for the sake of fun,
   Or just to hear the noise of their forty-four guns.

   And there's fire on the mountain, lightnin' in the air,
   Gold in them hills, and it's waitin' for me there.

4. Now my widow, she weeps by my grave;
   Tears flow free, for her man she couldn't save.
   Shot down in cold blood by a gun that carried fame,
   All for a useless and no-good worthless claim.

   And there's fire on the mountain, lightnin' in the air,
   Gold in them hills, and it's waitin' for me there.

   Reprise:

   Fire on the mountain, lightnin' in the air,
   Gold in them hills, and it's waitin' for me there,
   Waitin' for me there.

HAVE YOU EVER SEEN THE RAIN?

Words and Music by
John Fogerty

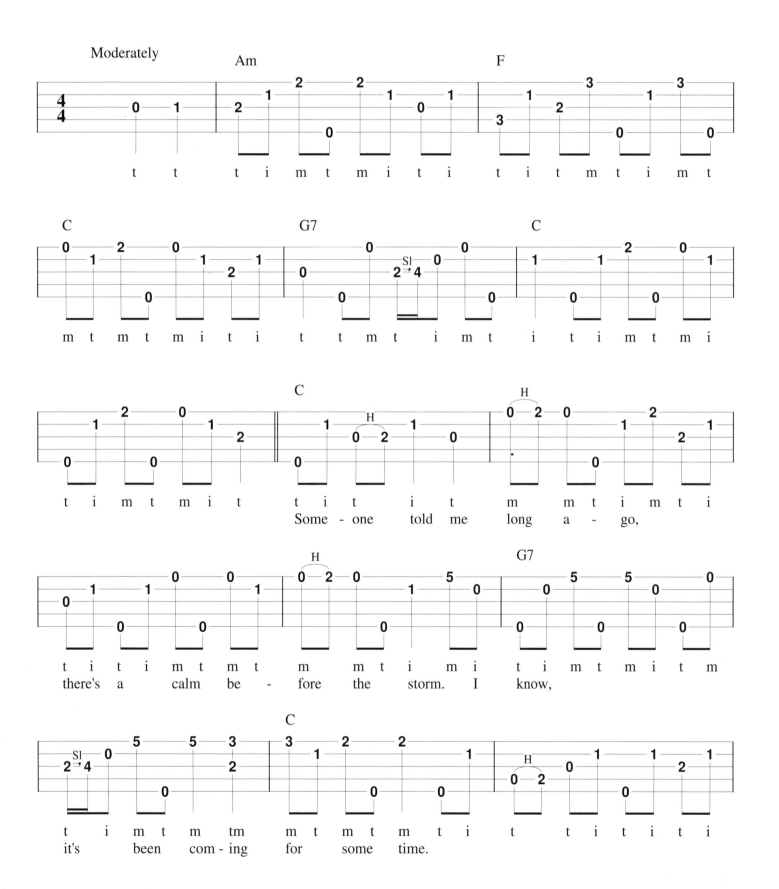

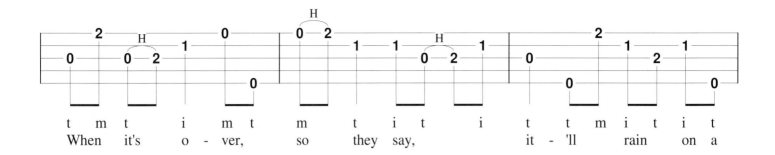

When it's o - ver, so they say, it - 'll rain on a

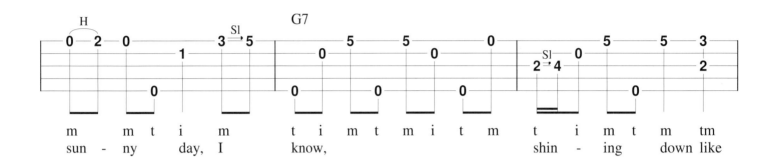

G7

sun - ny day, I know, shin - ing down like

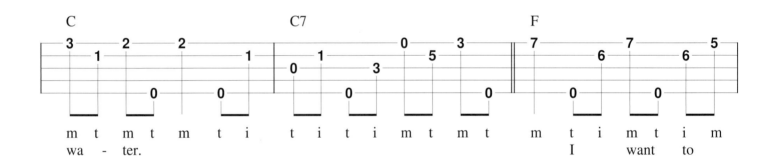

C   C7   F

wa - ter.   I   want to

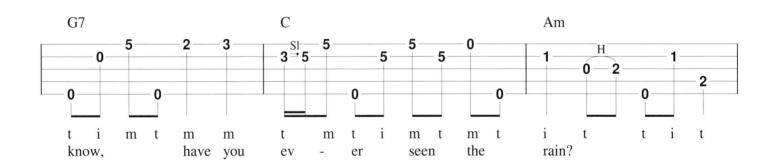

G7   C   Am

know,   have you ev - er seen the rain?

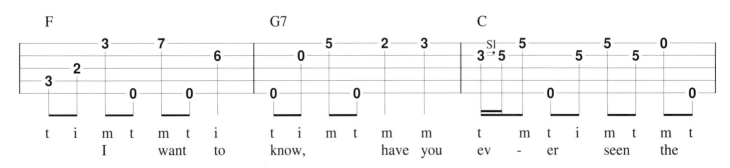

F   G7   C

I   want to know,   have you ev - er seen the

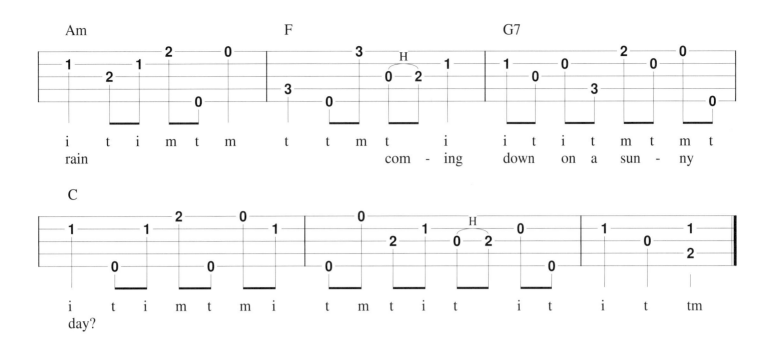

2. Yesterday and days before,
   Sun is cold and rain is hard.
   I know, been that way for quite some time.

   Till forever, on it goes,
   Through the circle of fast and slow.
   I know it can't stop, I wonder.

   Chorus

   I want to know,
   Have you ever seen the rain?
   I want to know,
   Have you ever seen the rain
   Coming down on a sunny day?

   Repeat Chorus

FOGGY MOUNTAIN BREAKDOWN

By Earl Scruggs

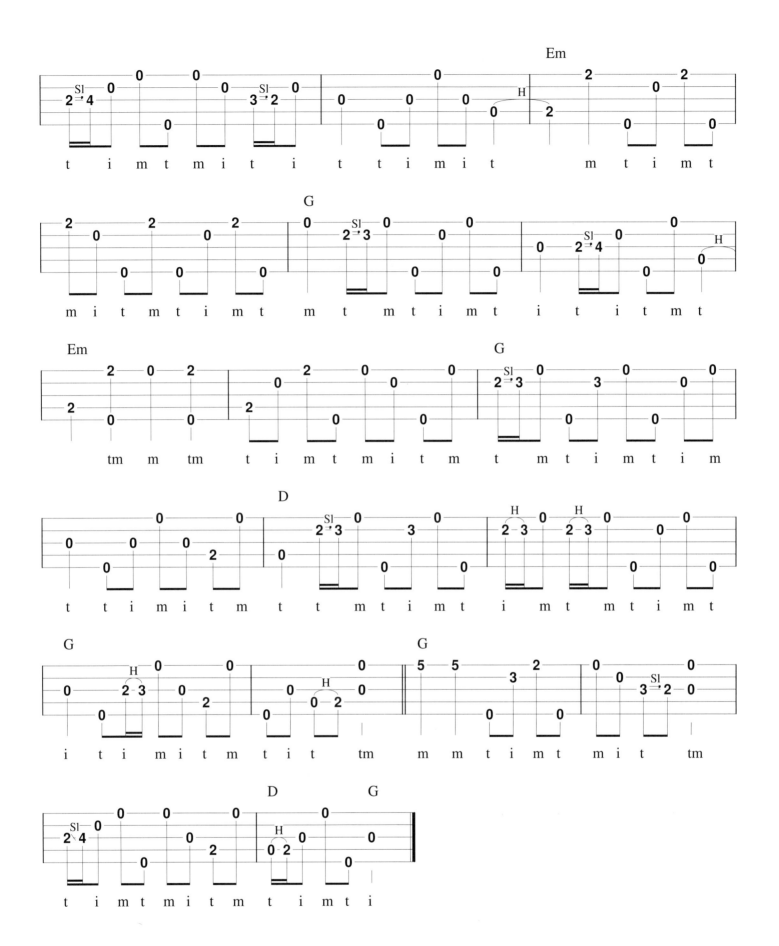

FOLLOW ME

Words and Music by
John Denver

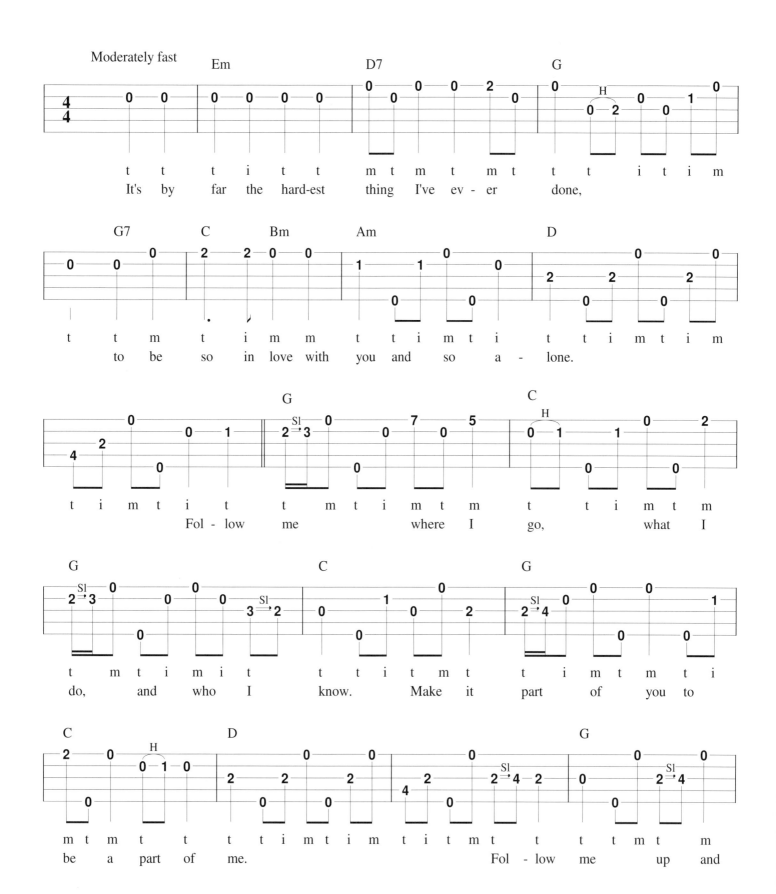

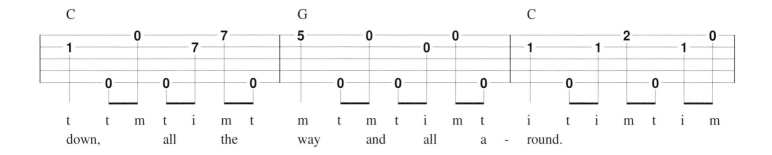

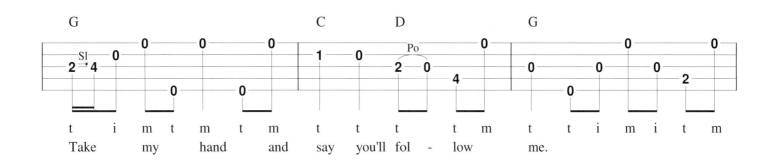

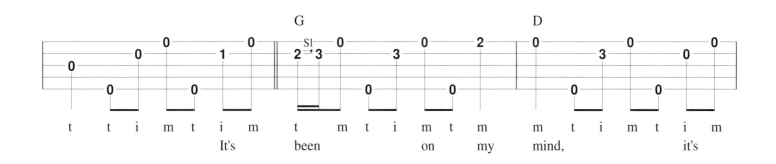

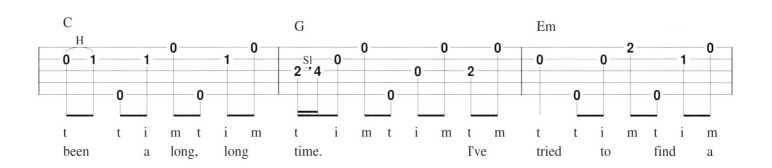

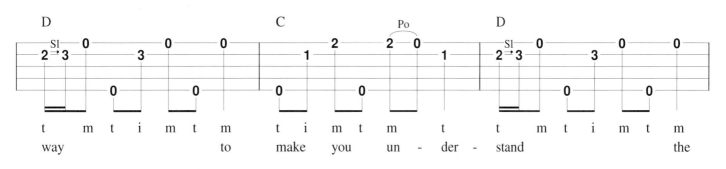

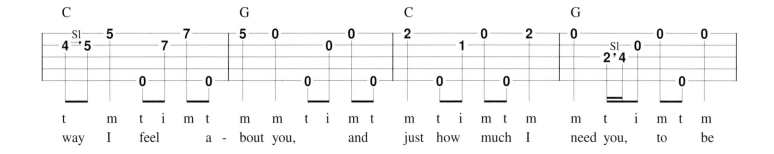

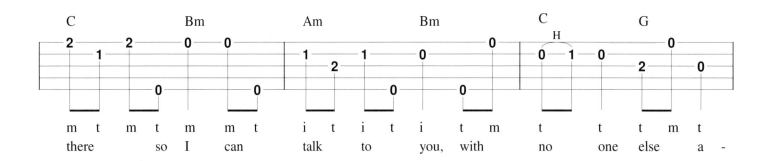

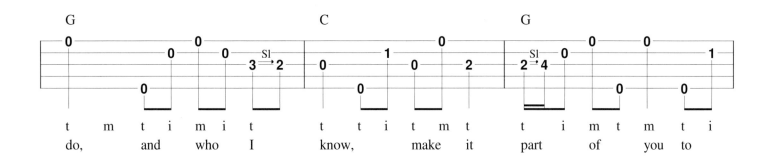

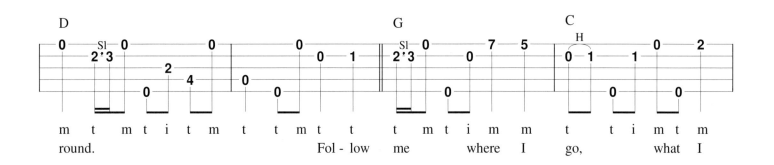

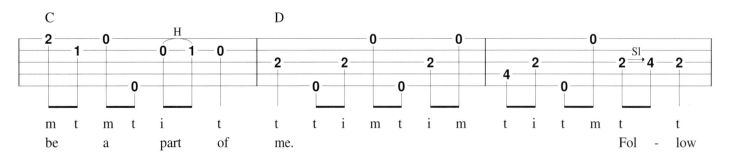

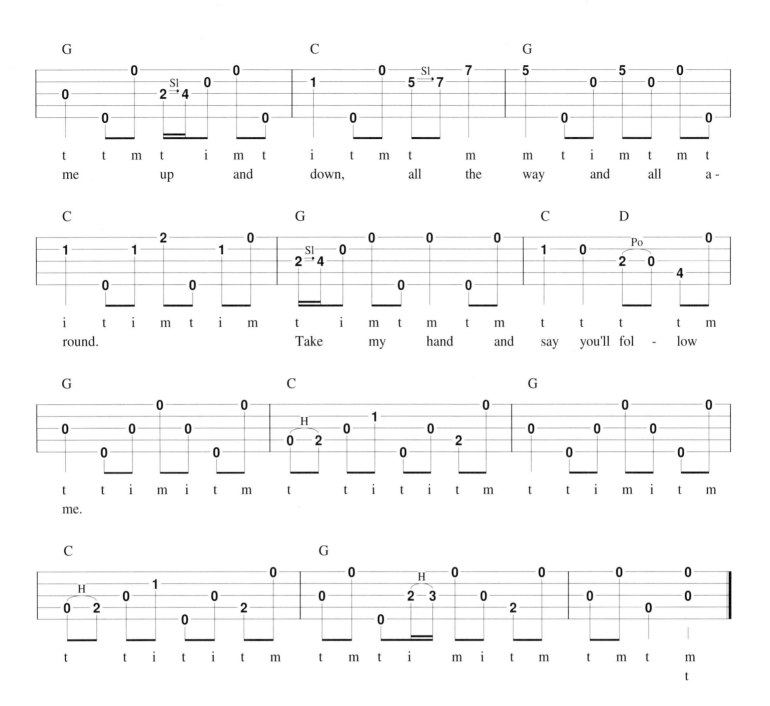

2. You see, I'd like to share my life with you and show you things I've seen,
   Places that I'm going to, places where I've been,
   To have you there beside me, and never be alone,
   And all the time that you're with me, we will be at home.

   to Chorus.

GARDEN SONG

Words and Music by
Dave Mallett

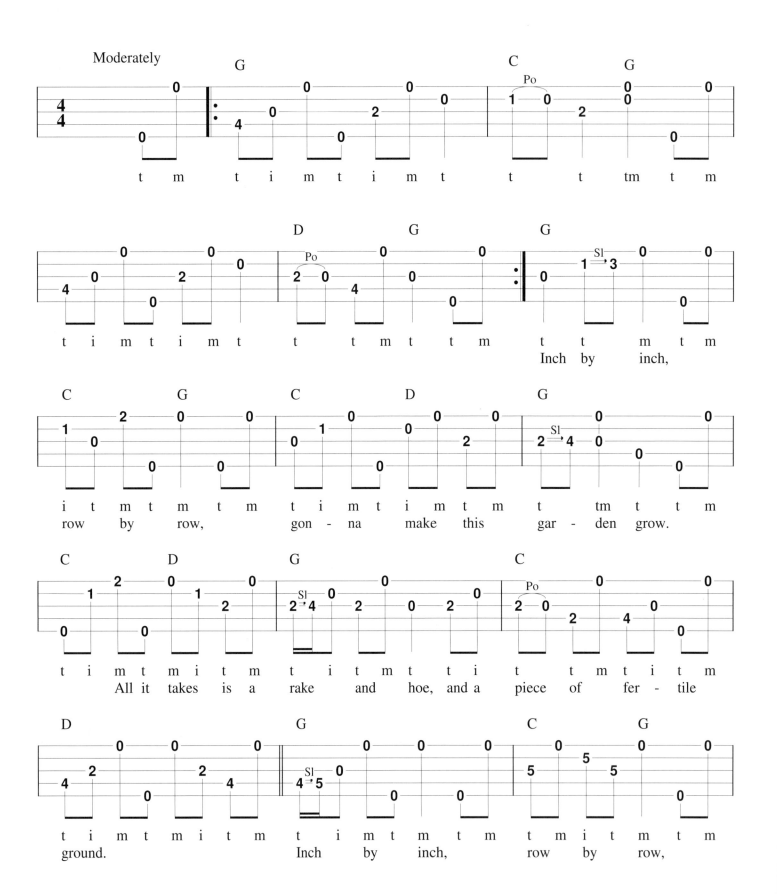

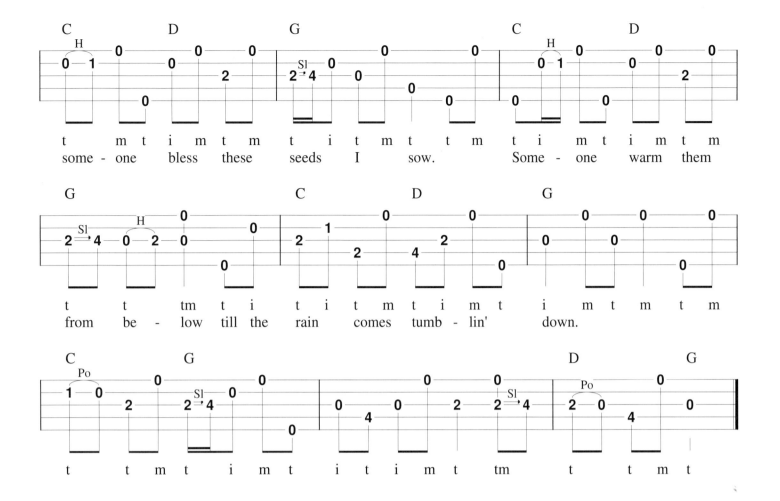

3. Pullin' weeds and pickin' stones,
   Man is made of dreams and bones.
   Feel the need to grow my own,
   'Cause the time is close at hand.

4. Rainful rain, sun and rain,
   Find my way in nature's chain.
   Tune my body and my brain,
   To the music from the land.

5. Plant your rows straight and long,
   Temper them with prayer and song.
   Mother Earth will make you strong
   If you give her love and care.

6. Old crow watchin' hungrily
   From his perch in yonder tree.
   In my garden I'm as free
   As that feathered thief up there.

GRANDFATHER'S CLOCK

By Henry Clay Work

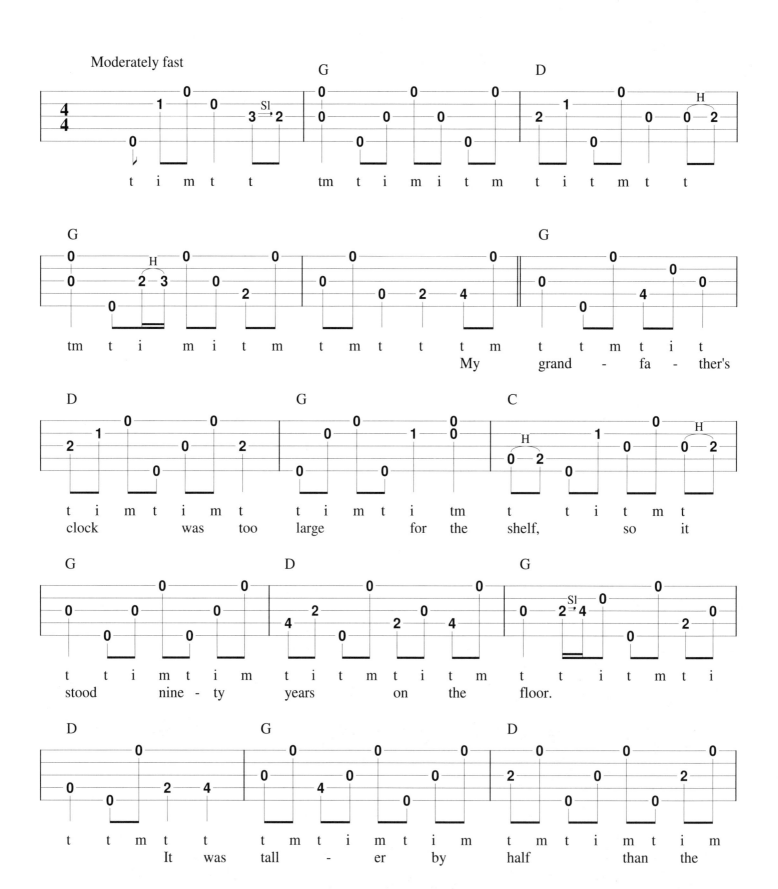

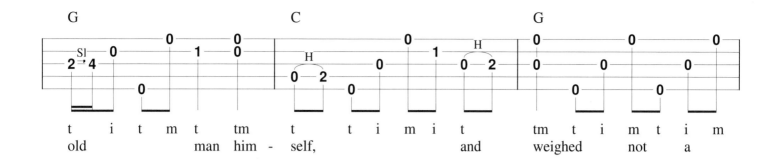

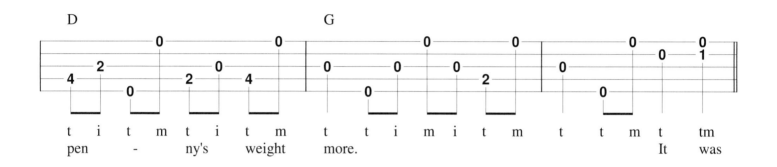

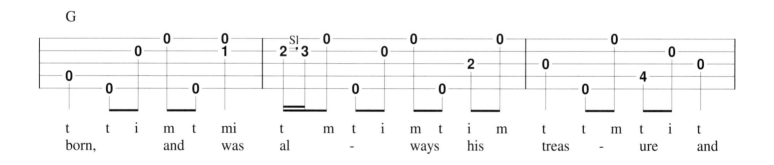

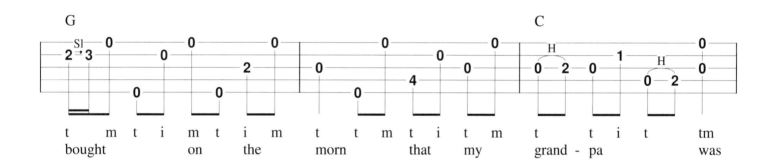

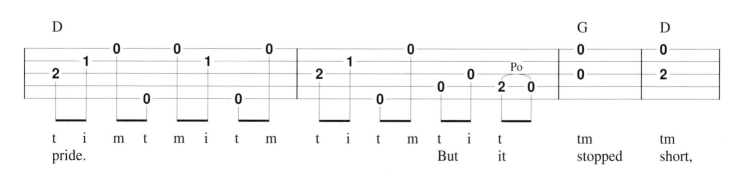

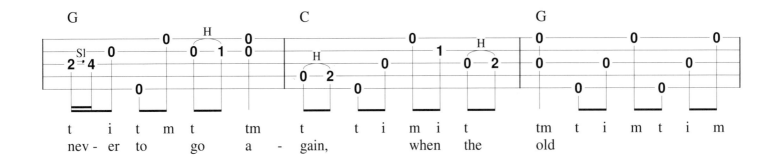

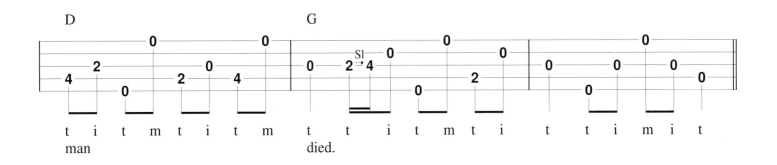

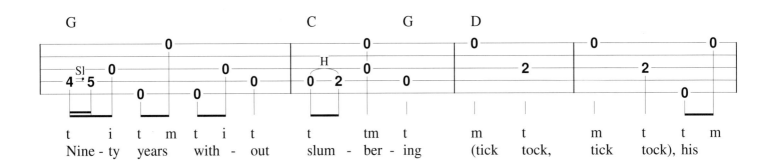

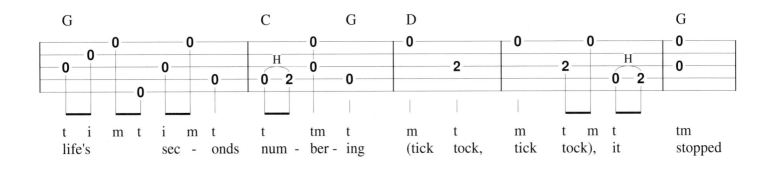

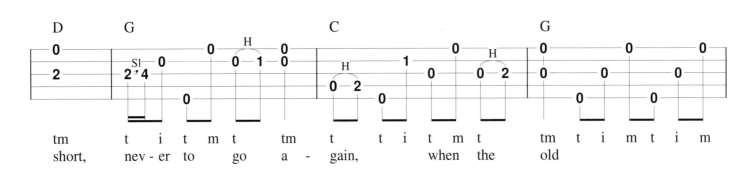

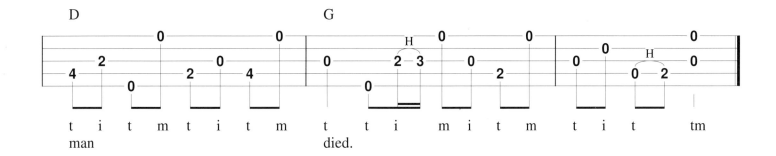

2. Watching its pendulum swing to and fro,
   Many hours he had spent as a boy.
   As he grew into manhood the clock seemed to know,
   For it shared every sorrow and joy.

   And it struck twenty-four as he entered the door
   With his beautiful and blushing bride.
   But it stopped short, never to go again,
   When the old man died.

3. My grandfather said that of those he could hire,
   Not a servant so faithful he'd found.
   For it wasted no time and it had but one desire,
   At the close of each week to be wound.

   Yes, it kept in its place, but not a frown upon its face,
   And its hands never hung by its side.
   But it stopped short, never to go again,
   When the old man died.

4. Then it rang an alarm in the dead of the night,
   An alarm that for years had been dumb.
   And we knew that his spirit was pluming for flight,
   That his hour for departure had come.

   Yes the clock kept the time, with a soft and muffled chime,
   As we stood there and watched by his side.
   But it stopped short, never to go again,
   When the old man died.

I CAN'T HELP BUT WONDER
(Where I'm Bound)

Words and Music by
Tom Paxton

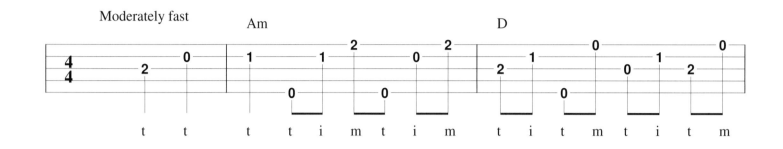

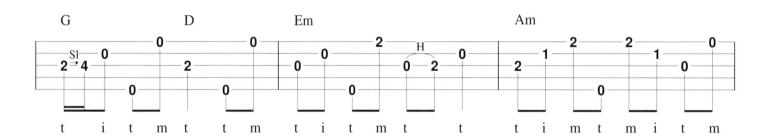

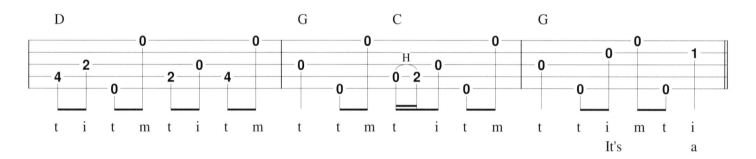

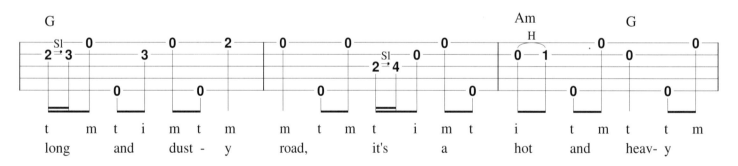

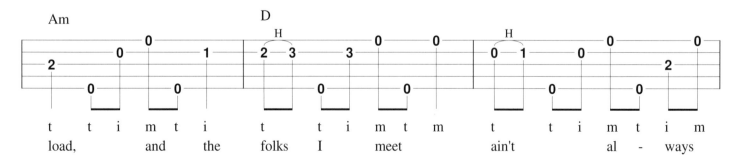

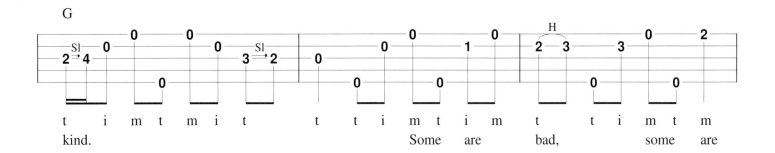

kind.   Some   are   bad,   some are

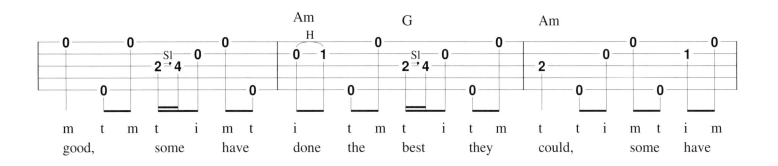

good,   some have   done the   best they   could,   some have

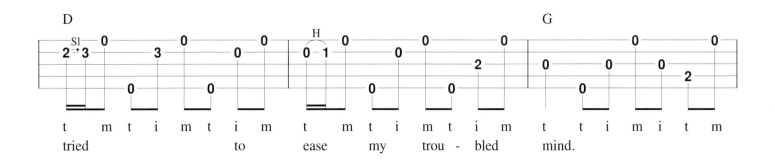

tried   to   ease   my   trou - bled   mind.

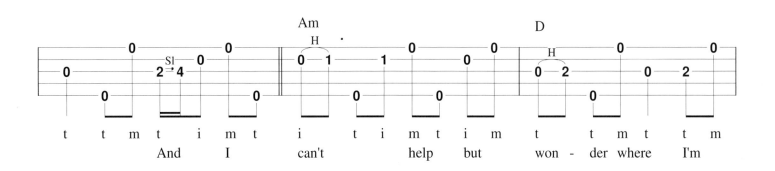

And   I   can't   help   but   won - der where   I'm

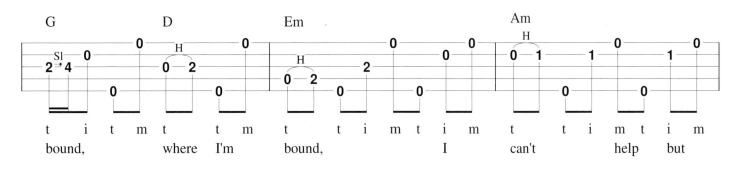

bound,   where I'm   bound,   I   can't   help   but

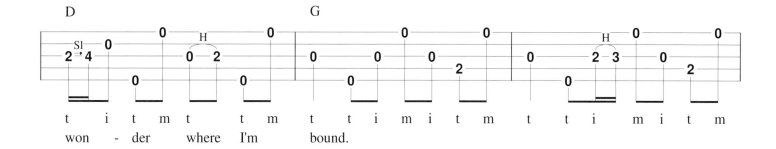

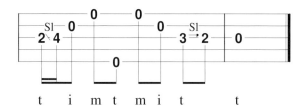

1. Well, I've been around this land, just a-doin' the best I can,
   Tryin' to find what I was meant to do.
   The faces that I see look as worried as can be,
   And it looks like they are a-wonderin' too.

   Refrain:
   And I can't help but wonder where I'm bound, where I'm bound,
   I can't help but wonder where I'm bound.

2. Well, I had a little girl one time, she had lips like sherry wine,
   And she loved me till my head went plumb insane.
   But I was too blind to see she was drifting away from me,
   And my good gal went off on a morning train.

   Repeat Refrain

3. I had a buddy way back home, but he started out to roam,
   And I hear he's out by Frisco bay.
   Sometimes when I've had a few, his old voice comes singin' through,
   And I'm goin' out to see him some old day.

   Repeat Refrain

4. If you see me passin' by, and you sit and wonder why,
   And you wish that you were a rambler too,
   Nail your shoes to the kitchen floor, lace 'em up and bar the door,
   And thank the stars for the roof that's over you.

   Repeat Refrain

I'LL FLY AWAY

Words and Music by
Albert E. Brumley

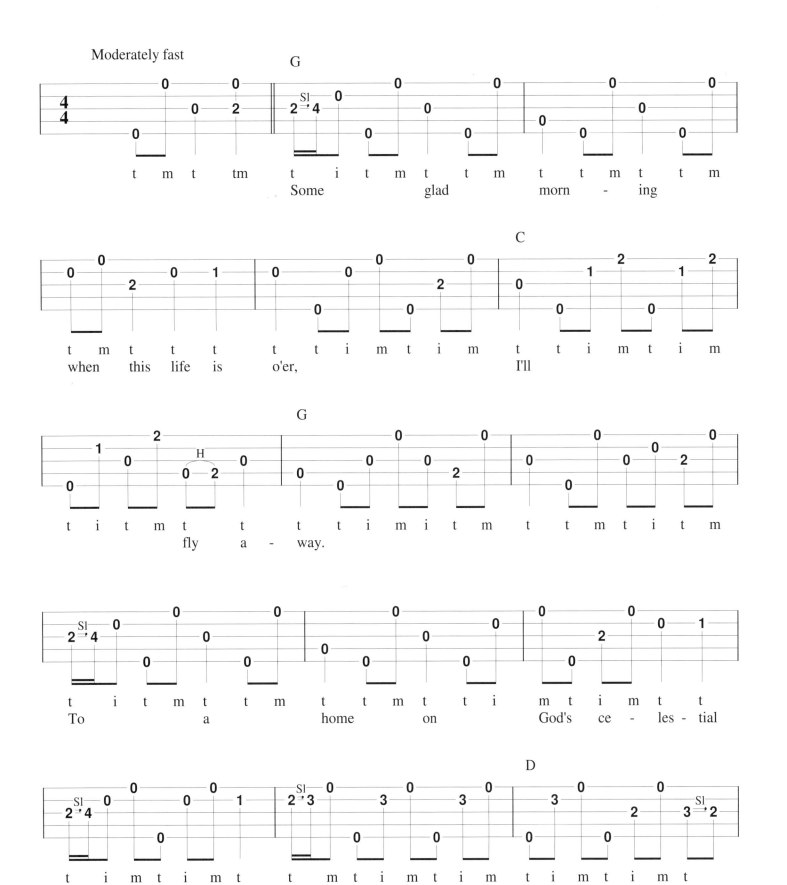

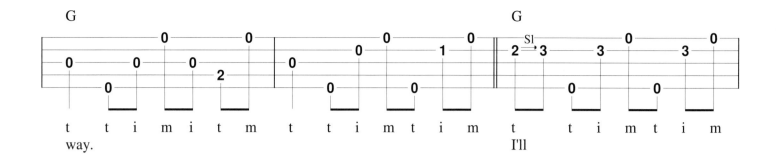

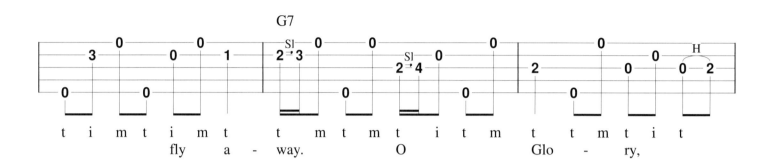

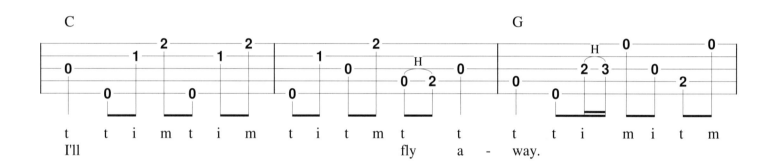

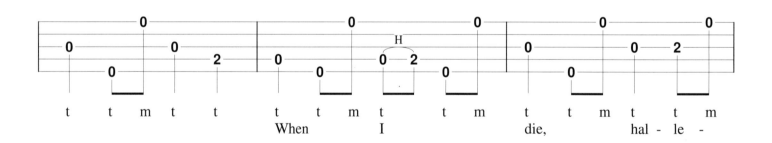

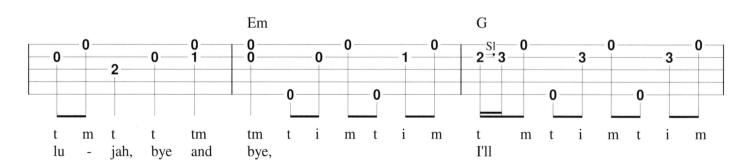

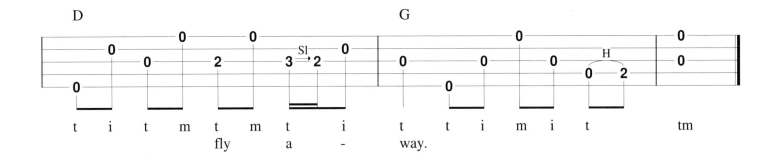

2. When the shadows of this life are gone, I'll fly away.
   Like a bird from prison bars has flown, I'll fly away.

   Chorus

   I'll fly away, O Glory, I'll fly away.
   When I die, hallelujah, bye and bye, I'll fly away.

3. Just a few more weary days and then, I'll fly away.
   To a land where joy shall never end, I'll fly away.

   Repeat Chorus

JAMAICA FAREWELL

Words and Music by
Irving Burgie

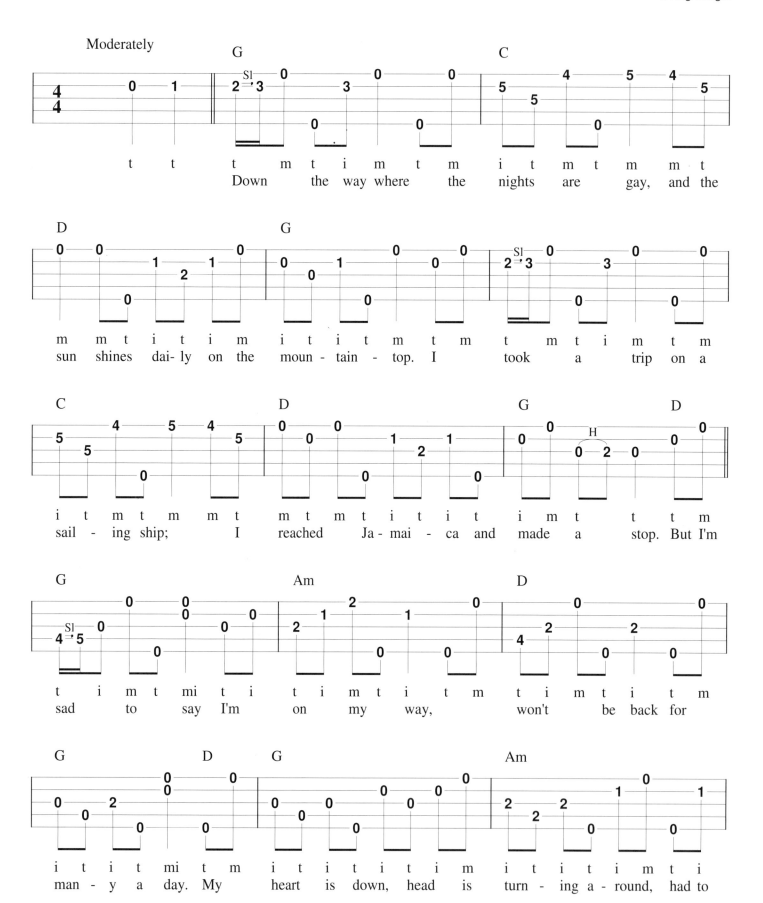

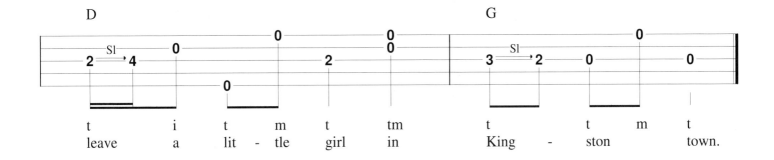

2. Down at the market you can hear
   Ladies cry out while on their heads they bear
   Ackie, rice, salt fish are nice,
   And the rum is fine any time of year.

   Chorus

   But I'm sad to say, I'm on my way,
   Won't be back for many a day.
   My heart is down, my head is turning around,
   I had to leave a little girl in Kingston Town.

3. Sounds of laughter everywhere,
   And the dancing girls swaying to and fro.
   I must declare my heart is there,
   Though I've been from Maine to Mexico.

   Repeat Chorus

THE LAST THING ON MY MIND

Words and Music by
Tom Paxton

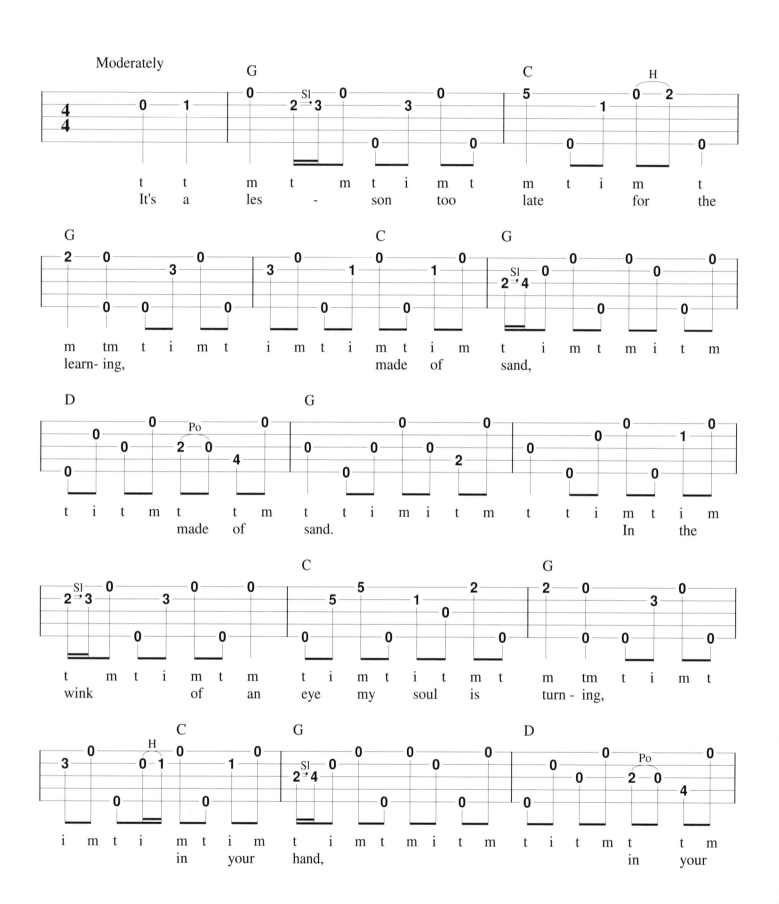

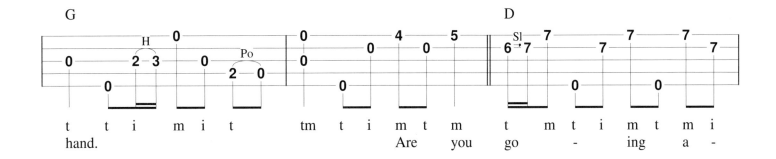

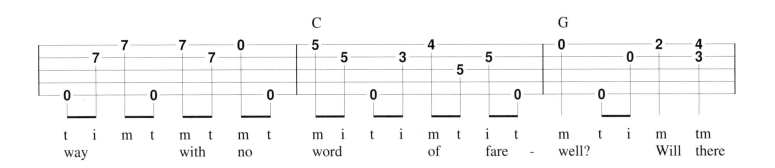

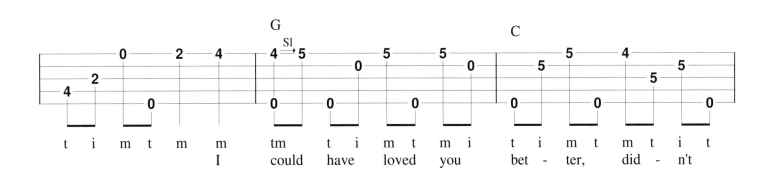

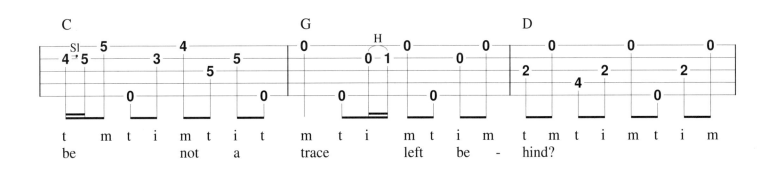

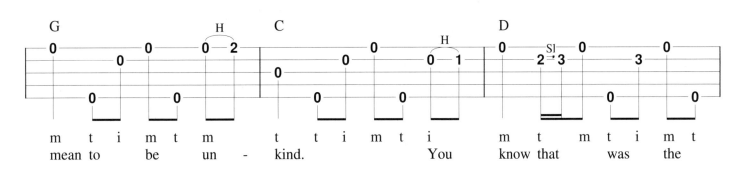

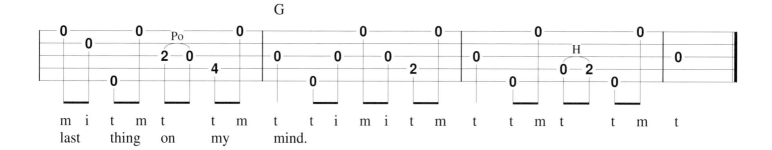

m i t m t   t m   t   t i m i t m   t   t m t   t m t

last thing on my   mind.

2. As I walk alone my thoughts are tumbling,
   'Round and 'round, 'round and 'round.
   Underneath our feet a subway's rumbling,
   Under ground, under ground.

   Chorus:

   Are you going away with no word of farewell?
   Will there be not a trace left behind?
   I could have loved you better, didn't mean to be unkind.
   You know that was the last thing on my mind.

3. You have reasons aplenty for going,
   This I know, this I know.
   The weeds have been steadily growing.
   Please don't go, please don't go.

   Repeat chorus

LEAVING ON A JET PLANE

Words and Music by
John Denver

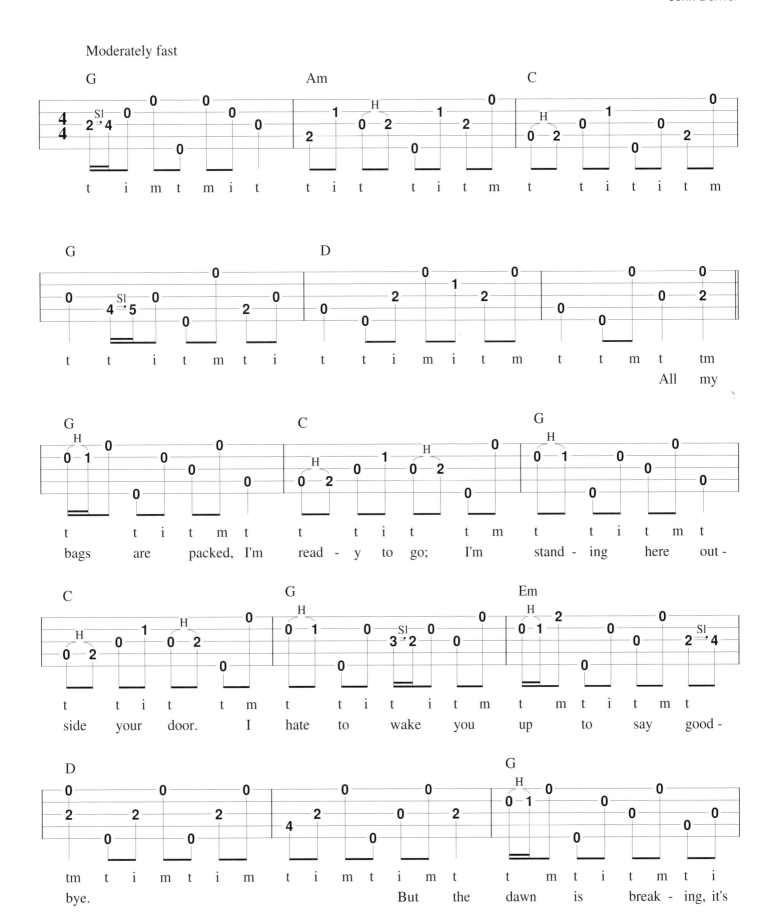

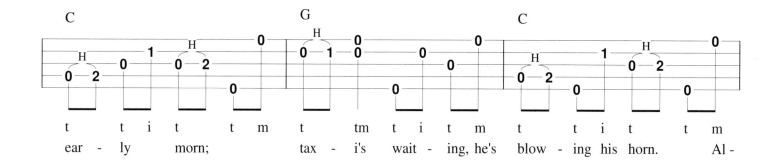

early morn; taxi's waiting, he's blowing his horn. Al-

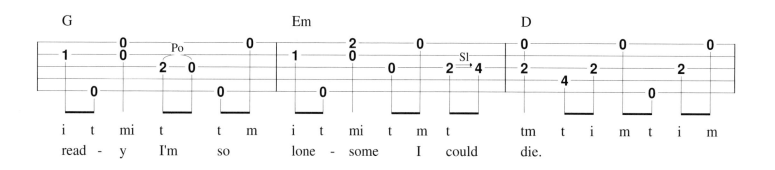

ready I'm so lonesome I could die.

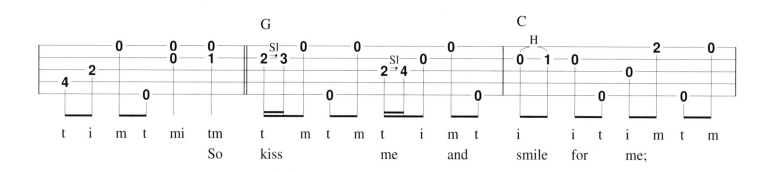

So kiss me and smile for me;

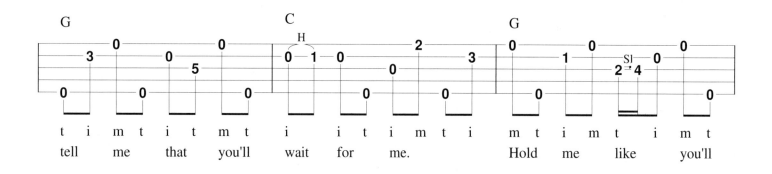

tell me that you'll wait for me. Hold me like you'll

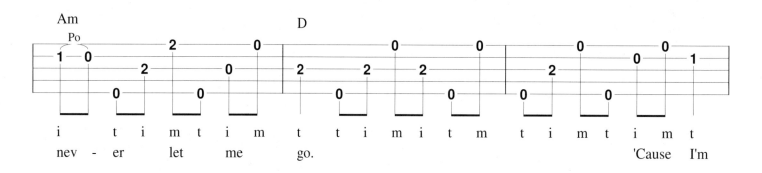

never let me go. 'Cause I'm

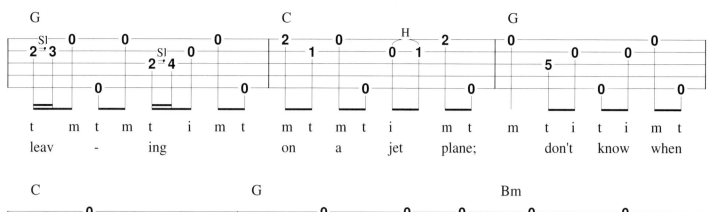

leav - ing   on   a   jet   plane;   don't   know   when

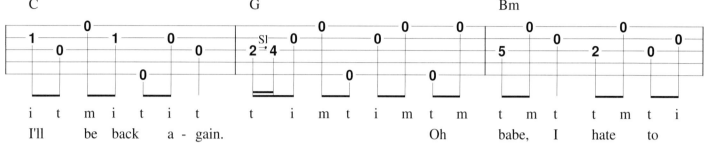

I'll   be   back   a - gain.   Oh   babe,   I   hate   to

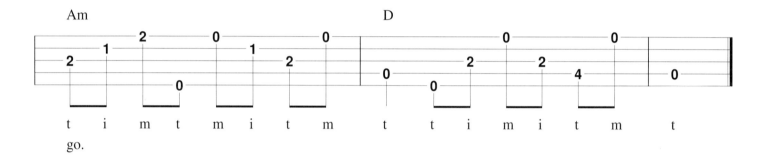

go.

2. There's so many times I've let you down, so many times I've played around.
   I tell you now, they don't mean a thing.
   Every place I go, I'll think of you; every song I sing, I'll sing for you.
   When I come back, I'll bring your wedding ring.

   Chorus

   So kiss me and smile for me; tell me that you'll wait for me.
   Hold me like you'll never let me go.
   'Cause I'm leaving on a jet plane; don't know when I'll be back again.
   Oh babe, I hate to go.

3. Now the time has come to leave you; one more time let me kiss you.
   Close your eyes and I'll be on my way.
   Dream about the days to come, when I won't have to leave alone,
   About the times, I won't have to say:

   Repeat Chorus

LOOKIN' OUT MY BACK DOOR

Words and Music by
John Fogerty

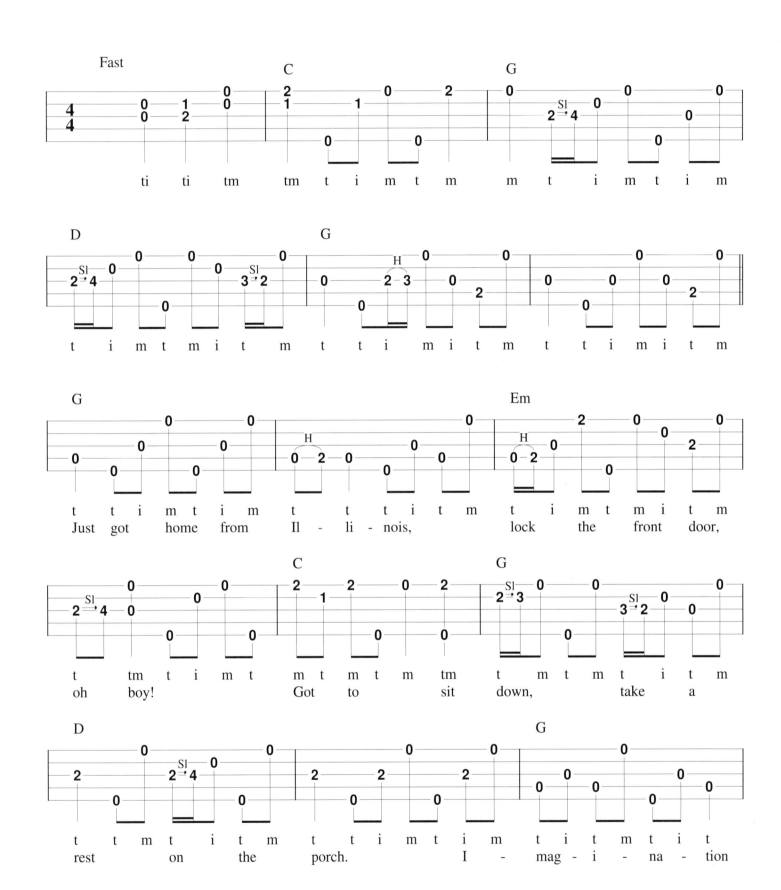

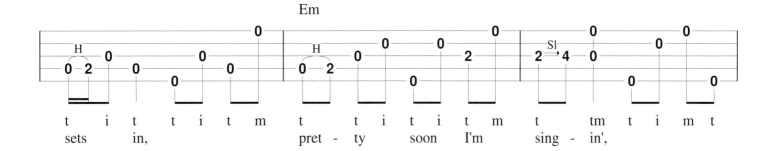

sets in,   pret - ty soon I'm sing - in',

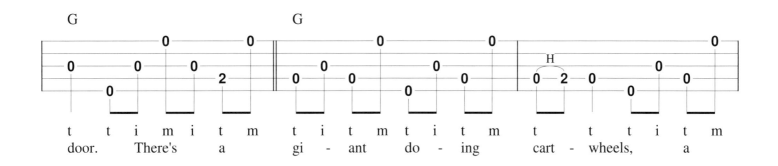

doo, doo, doo, look - in' out my back

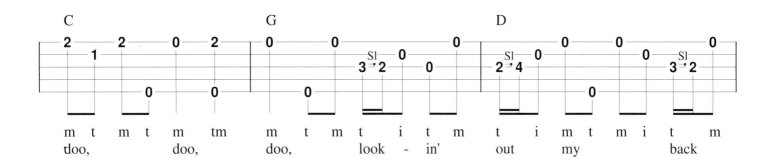

door. There's a gi - ant do - ing cart - wheels, a

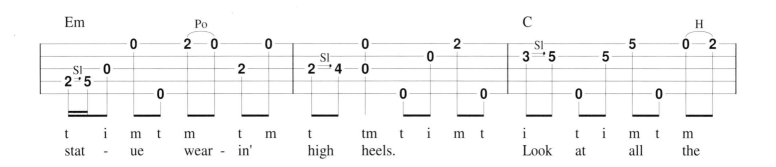

stat - ue wear - in' high heels. Look at all the

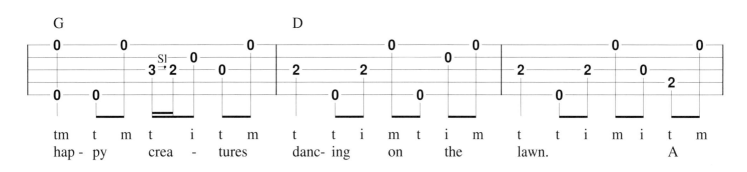

hap - py crea - tures danc- ing on the lawn. A

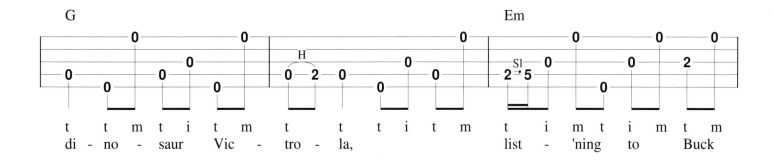

di - no - saur Vic - tro - la,   list - 'ning to Buck

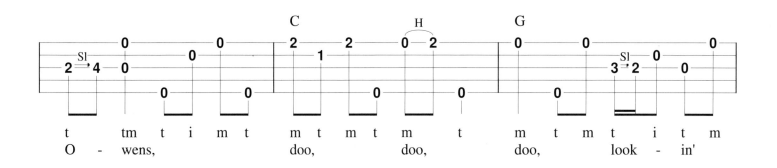

O - wens,   doo,   doo,   doo,   look - in'

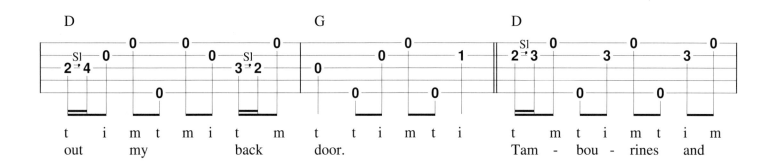

out   my   back   door.   Tam - bou - rines   and

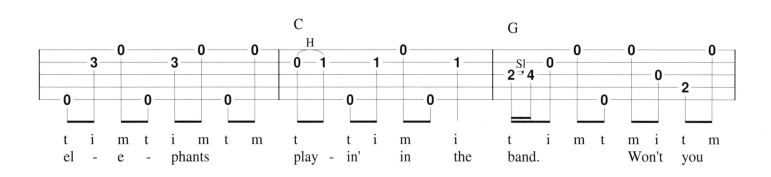

el - e - phants   play - in'   in   the   band.   Won't you

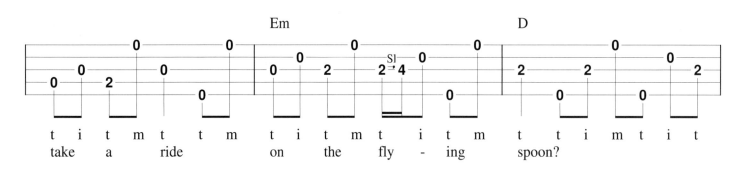

take   a   ride   on   the   fly - ing   spoon?

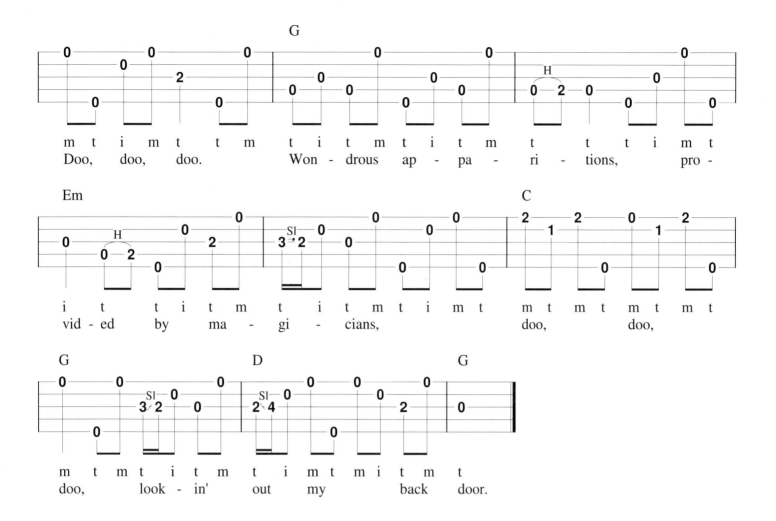

Second Chorus

Tambourines and elephants are playing in the band.
Won't you take a ride on the flyin' spoon? Doo, doo doo.
Bother me tomorrow; today, I'll buy no sorrows.
Doo, doo, doo, lookin' out my back door.

Third Chorus

Forward troubles Illinois, lock the front door, oh boy!
Look at all the happy creatures dancing on the lawn.
Bother me tomorrow; today, I'll buy no sorrows.
Doo, doo, doo, lookin' out my back door.

THE MARVELOUS TOY

Words and Music by
Tom Paxton

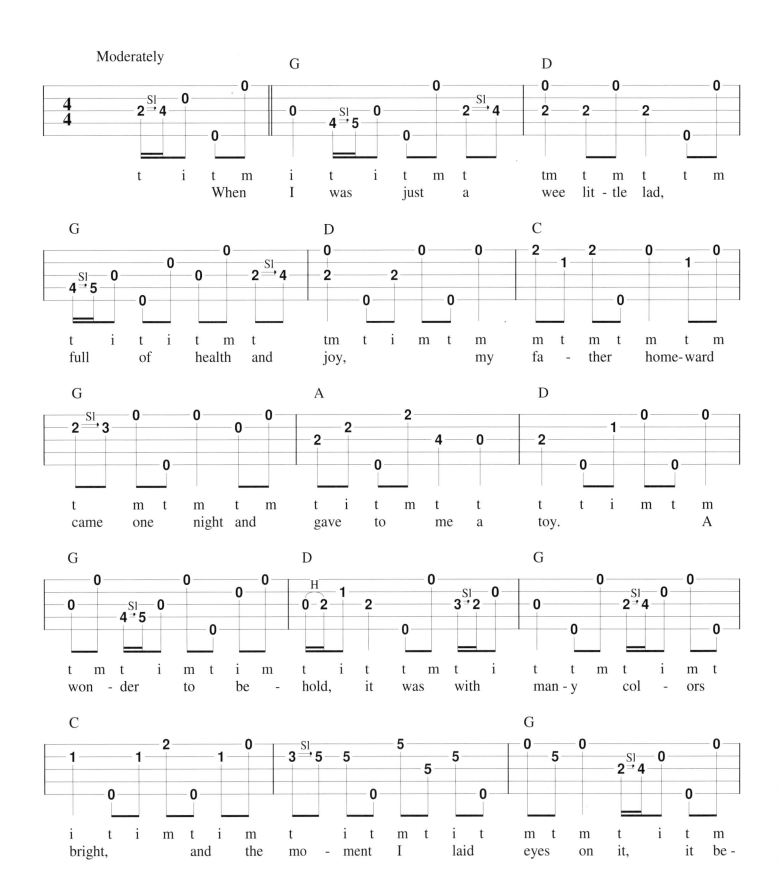

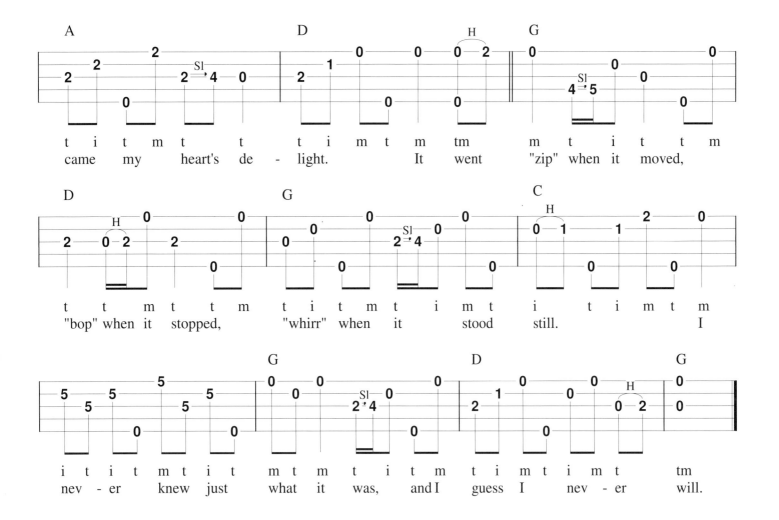

2. The first time that I picked it up, I had a big surprise,
   'Cause right on the bottom were two big buttons that looked like big green eyes.
   I pushed one and then the other, then twisted its lid; when I set it down again, here's what it did:

   Refrain:
   It went "zip" when it moved, and "bop" when it stopped, and "whirrr" when it stood still.
   I never knew just what it was and I guess I never will.

3. It first marched left and then marched right and then marched under a chair.
   And when I looked where it had gone, it wasn't even there.
   I started to cry, but my daddy laughed 'cause he knew that I would find,
   When I turned around my marvelous toy would be chugging from behind.

4. The years have gone by too quickly it seems, I have my own little boy,
   And yesterday I gave to him my marvelous little toy.
   His eyes nearly popped right out of his head, and he gave a squeal of glee!
   Neither one of us knows just what it is, but he loves it just like me!   It still goes... (Repeat Refrain)

MOUNTAIN DEW

Traditional

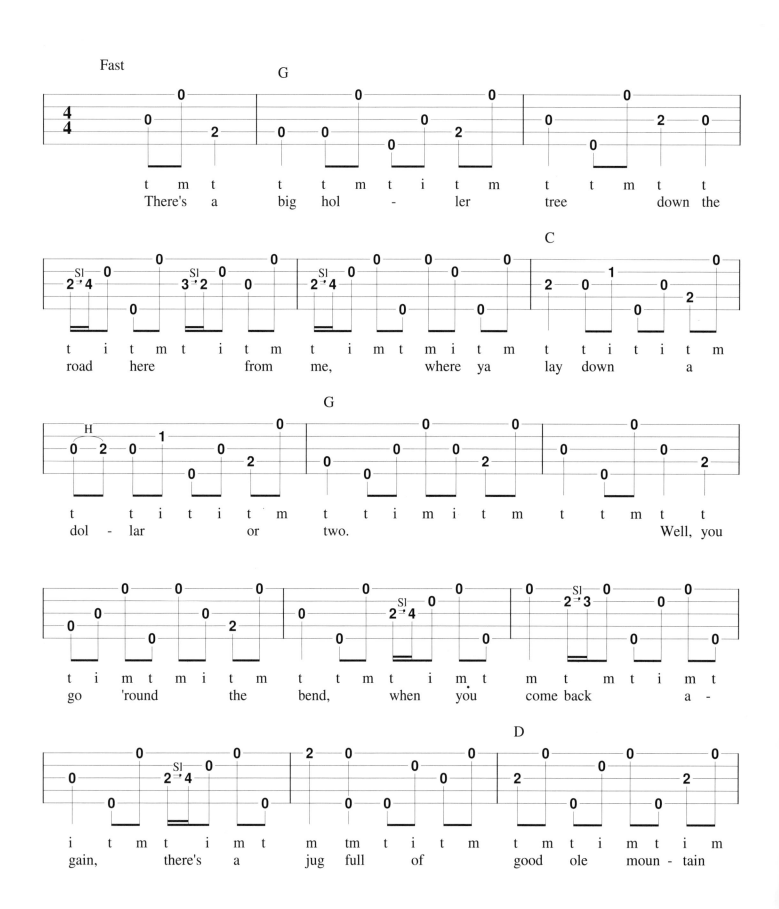

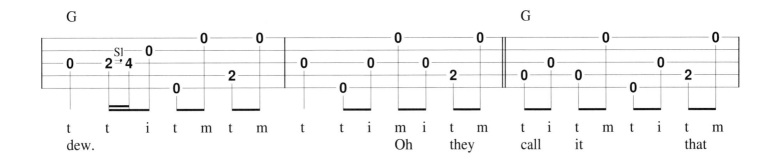

t t i t m t m t t i m i t m t i t m i t m
dew. Oh they call it that

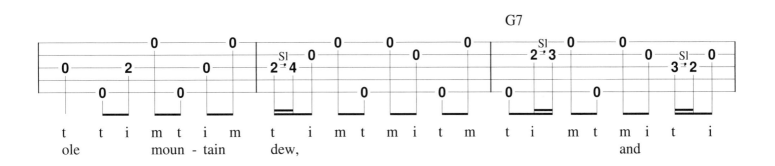

t t i m t i m t i m t m i t m t i m t m i t i
ole moun - tain dew, and

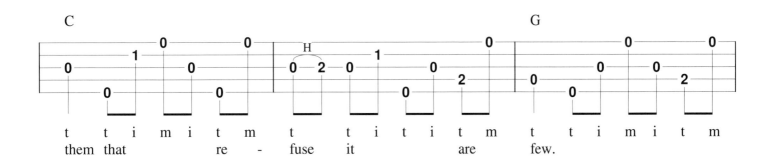

t t i m i t m t t i t i t m t t i m i t m
them that re - fuse it are few.

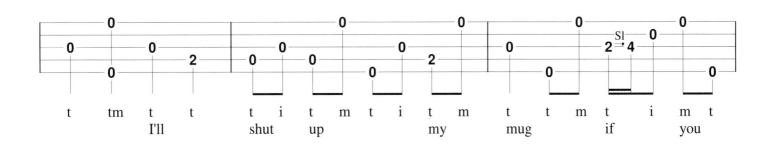

t tm t t t i t m t i t m t t m t i m t
I'll shut up my mug if you

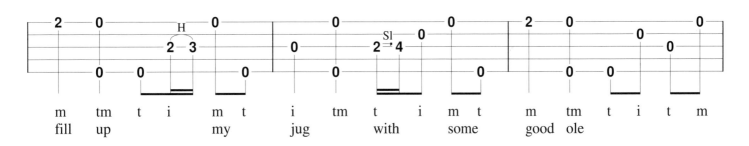

m tm t i m t i tm t i m t m tm t i t m
fill up my jug with some good ole

79

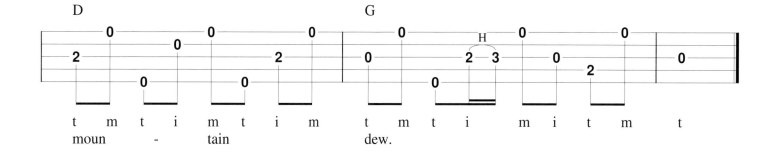

2. Now, my uncle Nort, he's sawed off and short;
   He measures about four foot two.
   But he thinks he's a giant when you give him a pint
   Of that good ole mountain dew.

3. Well, my ole aunt Jill bought some brand new perfume;
   It had such a sweet smellin' pew.
   But to her surprise, when she had it analyzed,
   It was nothin but good ole mountain dew.

   Chorus

   Oh they call it that ole mountain dew and them that refuse it are few.
   I'll shut up my mug if you fill up my jug with some good ole mountain dew.

4. Well, the preacher rolled by with his head heisted high,
   Said his wife had been down with the flu.
   And he thought that I ought just sell him a quart
   Of that good ole mountain dew.

5. Well, my brother Bill's got a still on the hill,
   Where he runs out a gallon or two.
   Now the buzzards in the sky get so drunk they can't fly
   From smellin' that good ole mountain dew.

   Repeat Chorus

MY RAMBLIN' BOY

Words and Music by
Tom Paxton

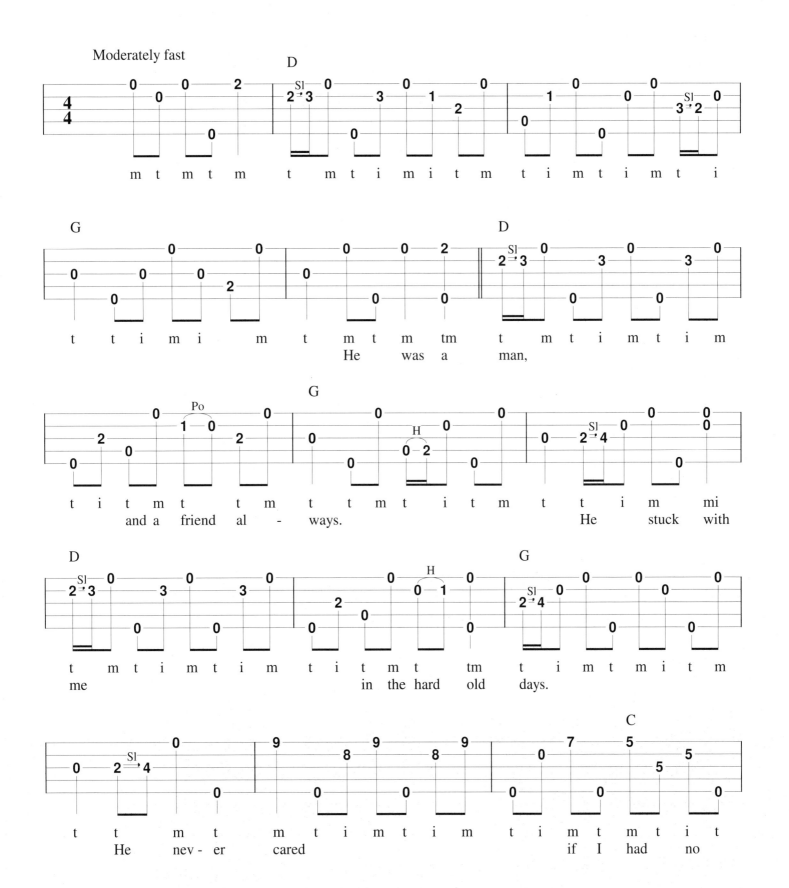

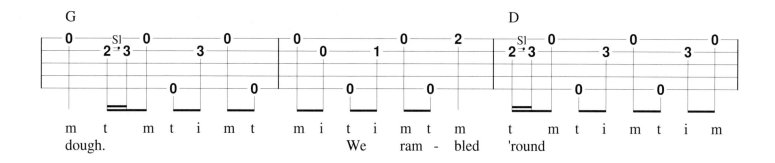

dough.   We ram - bled 'round

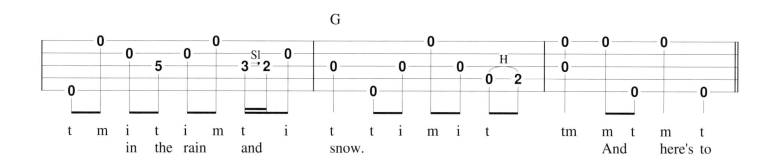

in the rain and snow.   And here's to

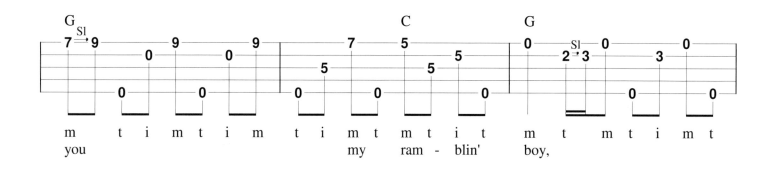

you   my ram - blin' boy,

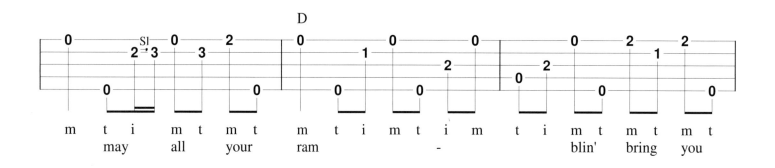

may all your ram -   blin' bring you

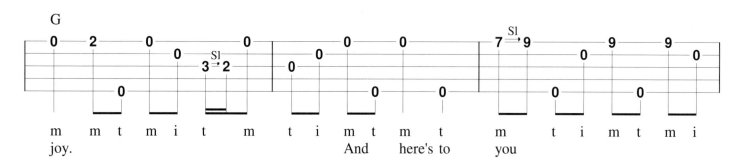

joy.   And here's to you

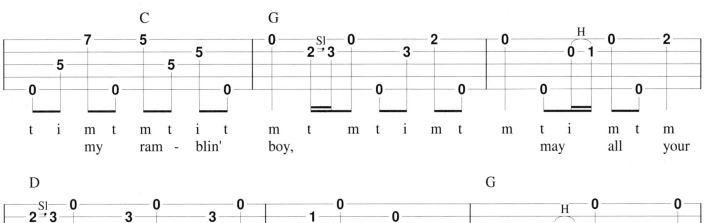

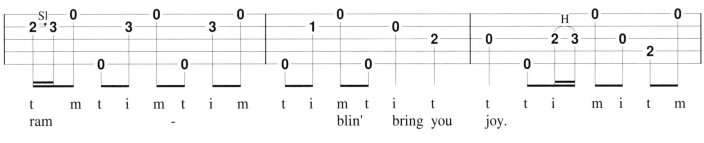

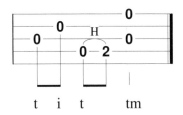

2. In Tulsa town we chanced to stray; we thought we'd try to work one day.
   The boss said he had room for one; says my old pal, "We'd rather bum!"

   Chorus

   And here's to you my ramblin' boy, may all your ramblin' bring you joy.
   And here's to you my ramblin' boy, may all your ramblin' bring you joy.

3. Late one night in a jungle camp, the weather it was cold and damp.
   He got the chills and he got 'em bad; they took the only friend I had.

   Repeat Chorus

4. He left me here to ramble on; my ramblin' pal is dead and gone.
   If when we die we go somewhere, I'll bet you a dollar he's ramblin' there.

   Repeat Chorus

SCARBOROUGH FAIR/CANTICLE

Arrangement and Original Counter Melody by
Paul Simon and Arthur Garfunkel

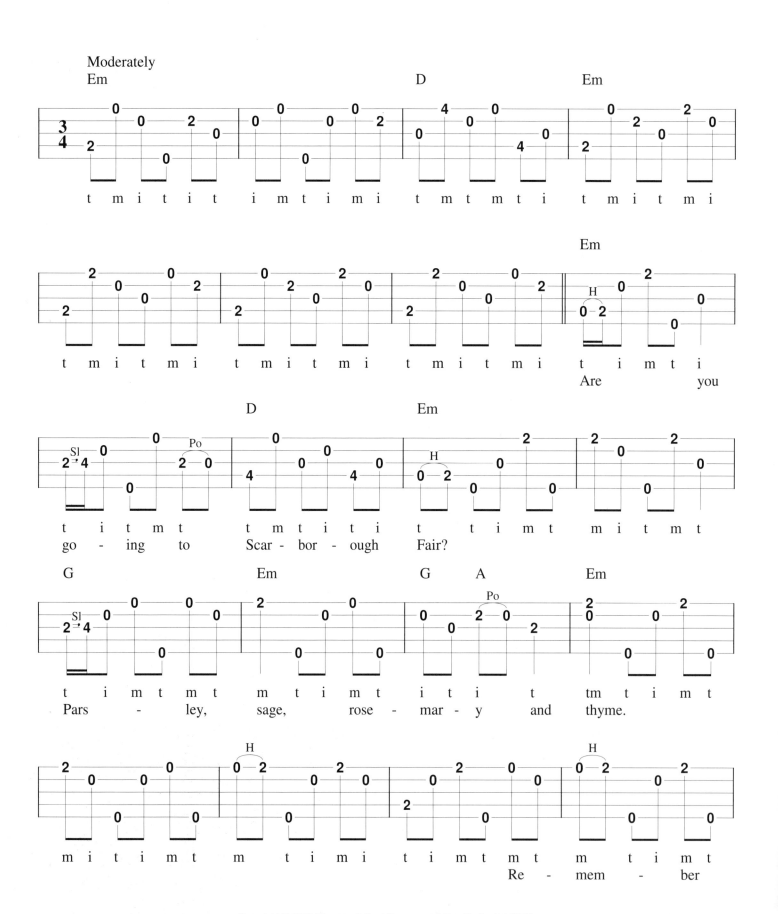

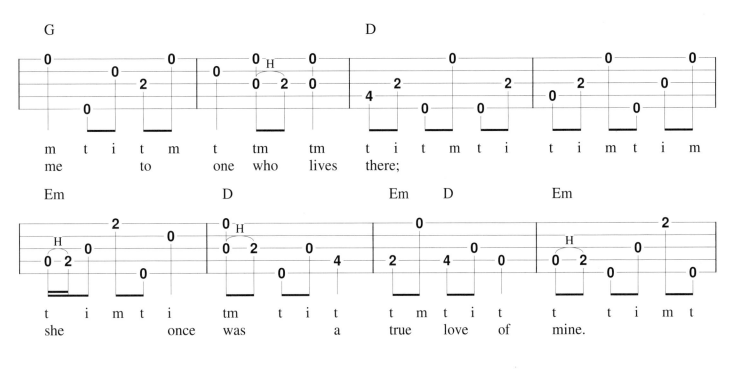

me to one who lives there;

she once was a true love of mine.

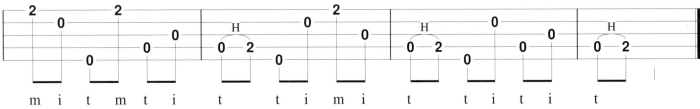

2. Tell him to make me a cambric shirt.
   Parsley, sage, rosemary and thyme.
   Without no seam nor needlework,
   Then he'll be a true love of mine.

3. Tell him to find me an acre of land.
   Parsley, sage, rosemary and thyme.
   Between the salt water and the sea strand,
   Then he'll be a true love of mine.

4. Are you going to Scarborough Fair?
   Parsley, sage, rosemary and thyme.
   Remember me to one who lives there;
   She once was a true love of mine.

SHADY GROVE

Appalachian Folk Song

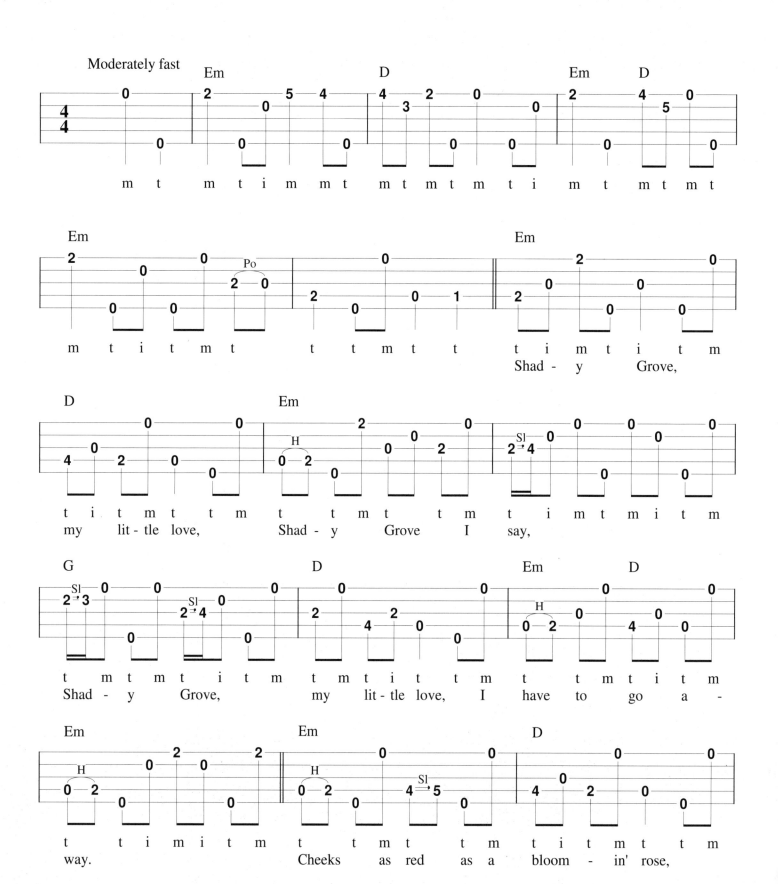

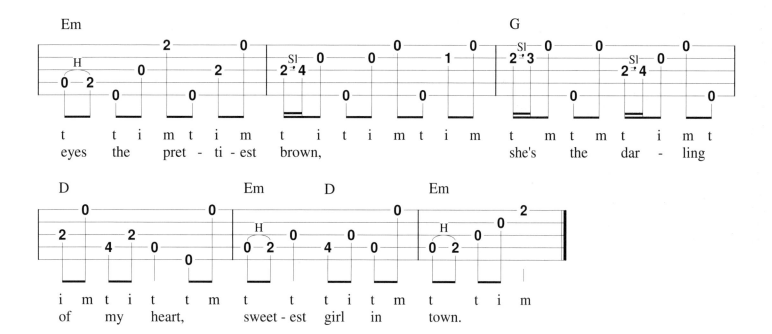

2. I wish I had a big fine horse, and corn to feed him on,
   And Shady Grove to stay at home, and feed him while I'm gone.
   Went to see my Shady Grove, she was standing at the door,
   Her shoes and stockings in her hand, and her bare feet on the floor.

   Chorus

   Shady Grove, my little love, Shady Grove I say,
   Shady Grove, my little love, I have to go away.

3. When I was a little boy, I wanted a Barlow knife,
   And now I want little Shady Grove to say she'll be my wife.
   A kiss from pretty little Shady Grove is sweet as brandy wine,
   And there ain't no girl in this old world that's prettier than mine.

   Repeat Chorus

TAKE ME HOME, COUNTRY ROADS

Words and Music by
John Denver, Bill Danoff
and Taffy Nivert

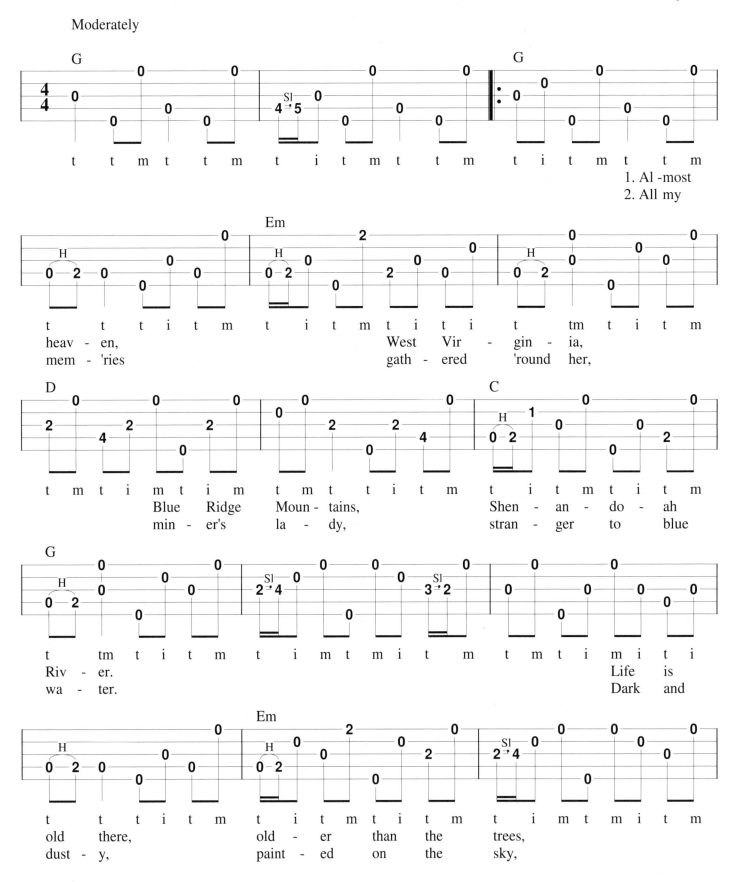

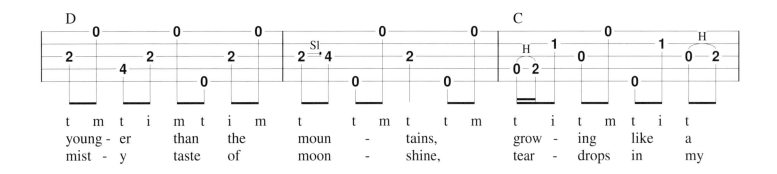

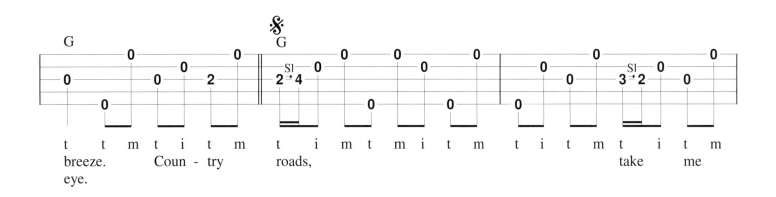

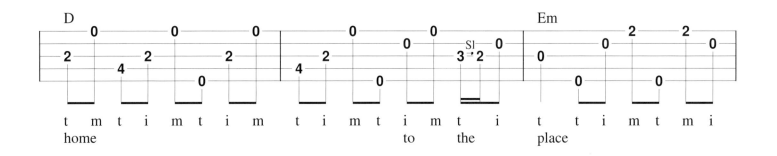

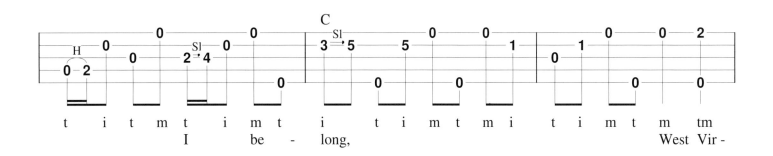

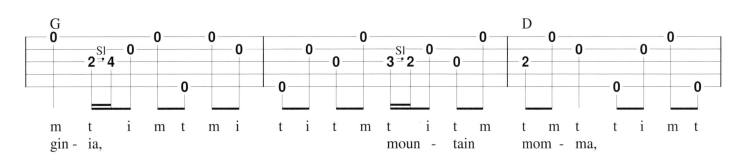

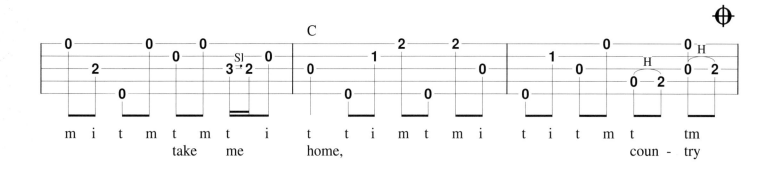

take me   home,   coun - try

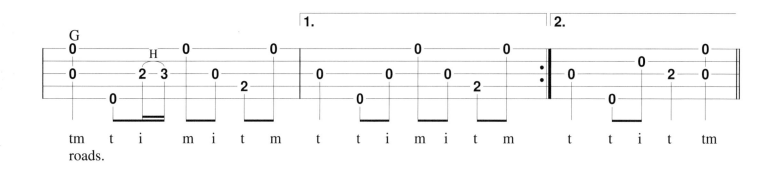

roads.

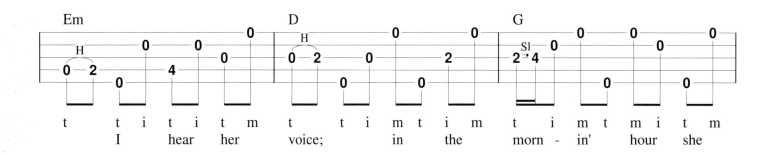

I   hear   her   voice;   in   the   morn - in'   hour   she

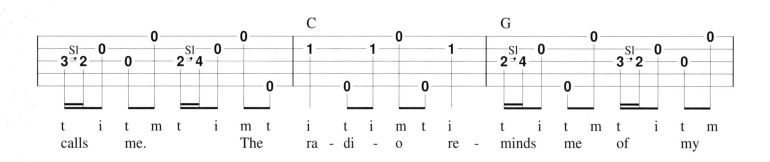

calls   me.   The   ra - di - o   re - minds   me   of   my

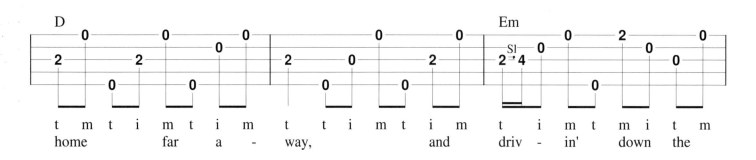

home   far   a -   way,   and   driv - in'   down   the

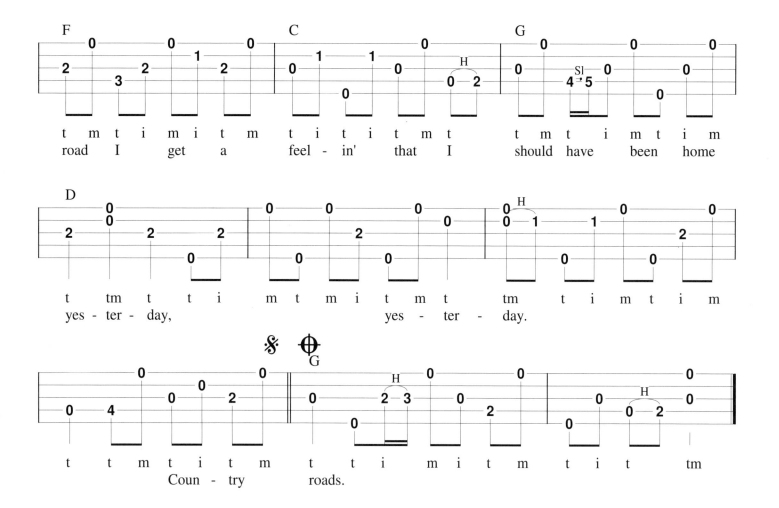

Chorus

Country Roads, take me home to the place I belong,
West Virginia, mountain momma, take me home, country roads.

Repeat Chorus

TEACH YOUR CHILDREN

Words and Music by
Graham Nash

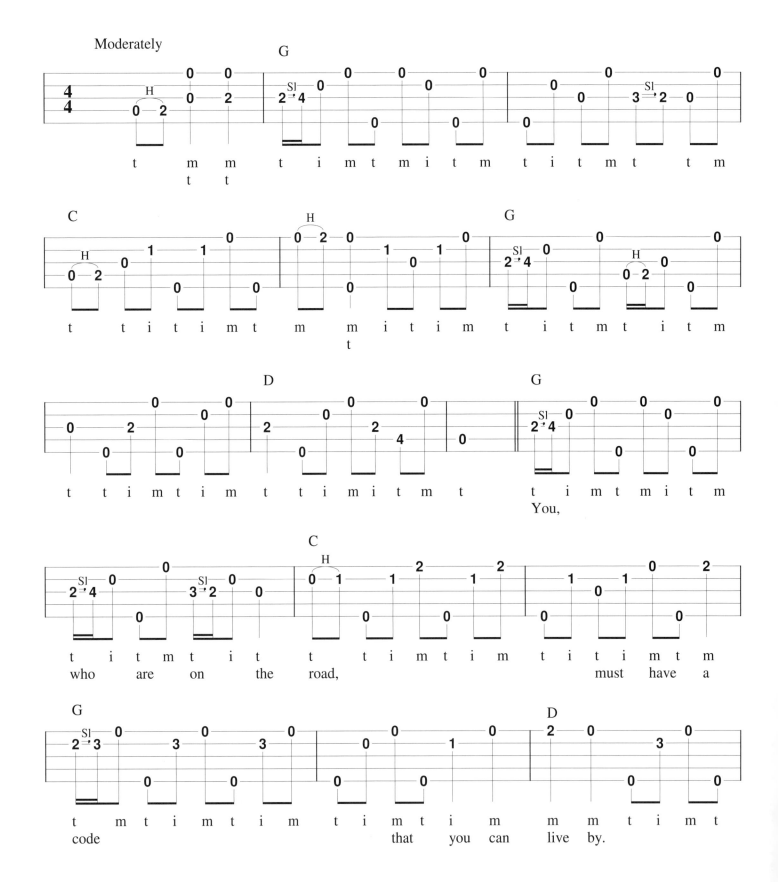

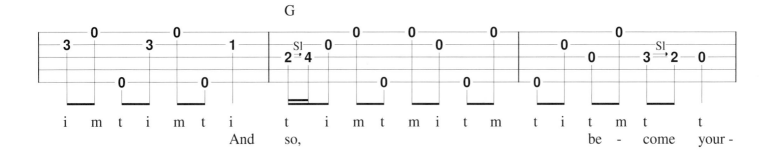

And so,   be - come your-

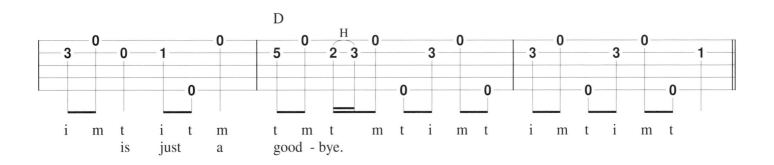

self,   'cause   the   past,

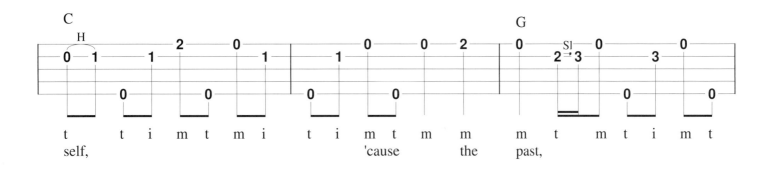

is   just   a   good - bye.

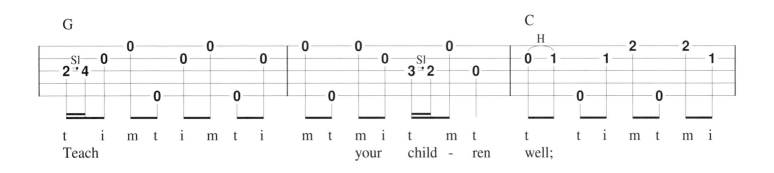

Teach   your child - ren well;

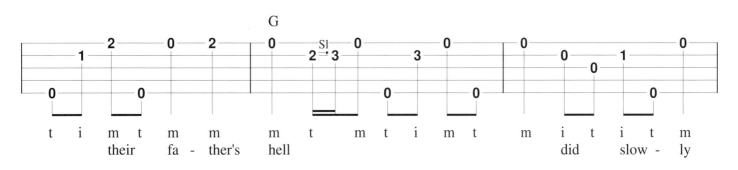

their fa - ther's hell   did   slow - ly

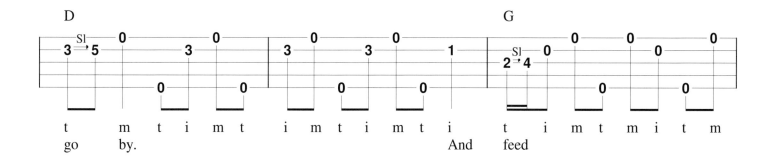

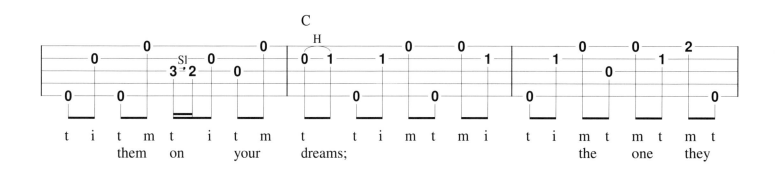

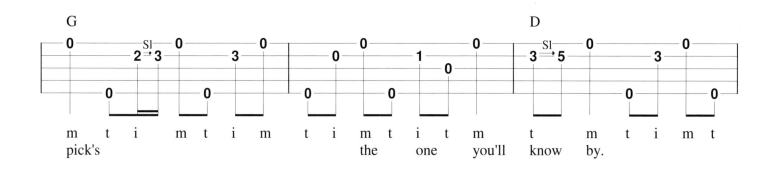

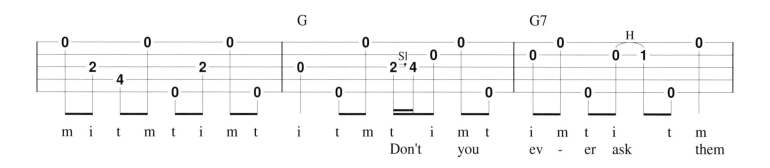

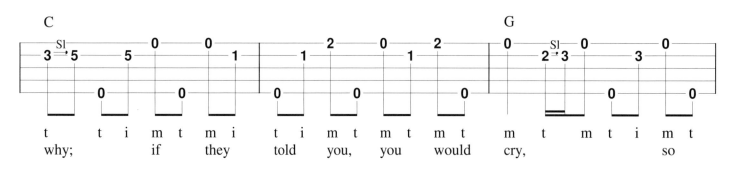

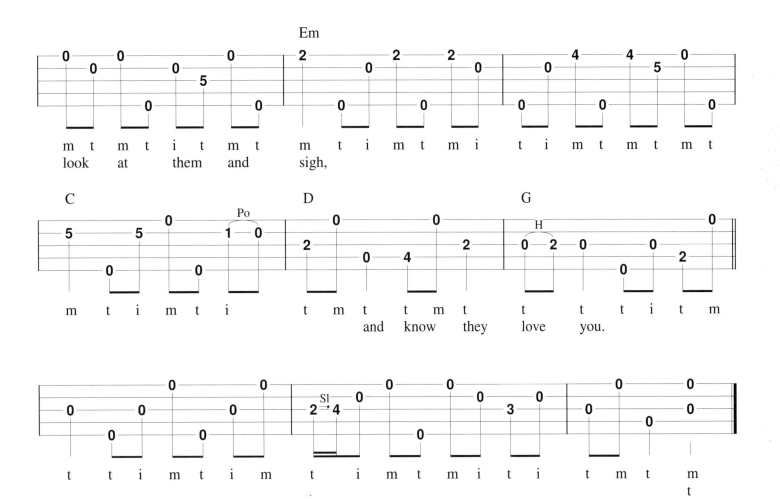

2. And you, of the tender years, can't know the fears that your elders grew by.
   And so, please help them with your youth; they seek the truth before they can die.
   Teach your parents well; their children's hell will slowly go by.
   And feed them on your dreams; the one they pick's the one you'll know by.
   Don't you ever ask them why; if they told you, you would cry,
   So just look at them and sigh, and know they love you.

THIS LAND IS YOUR LAND

Words and Music by
Woody Guthrie

Moderately fast

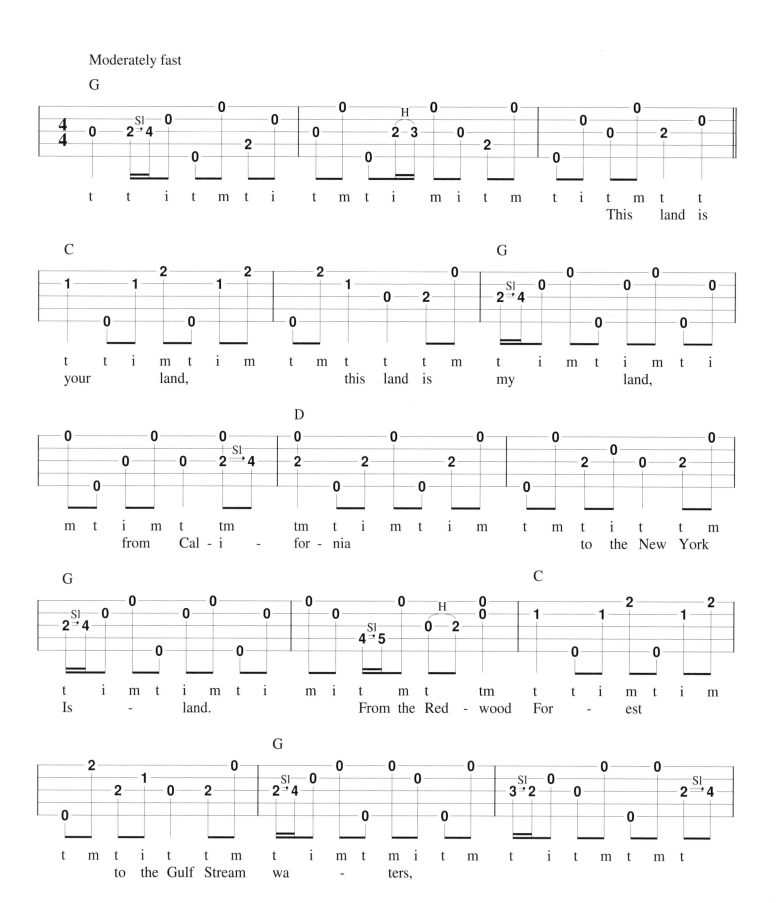

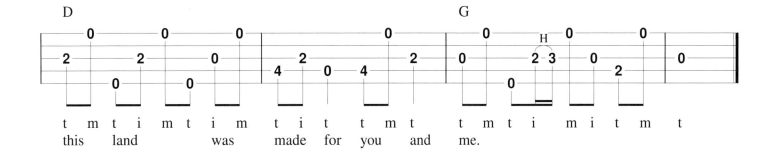

1. As I was walking a ribbon of highway,
   I saw above me an endless skyway.
   I saw below me a golden valley;
   This land was made for you and me.

   Chorus

   This land is your land, this land is my land,
   From California to the New York Island.
   From the Redwood Forest to the Gulf Stream waters,
   This land was made for you and me.

2. I've roamed and rambled, and followed my footsteps
   To the sparkling sands of her diamond deserts.
   And all around me a voice was sounding,
   This land was made for you and me.

   Repeat Chorus

3. The sun comes shining as I was strolling,
   The wheat fields waving, and the dust clouds rolling.
   The fog was lifting, a voice come chanting,
   This land was made for you and me.

   Repeat Chorus

4. As I was walking, I saw a sign there,
   And that sign said "no trespassing."
   But on the other side, it didn't say nothin!
   Now, that side was made for you and me!

   Repeat Chorus

5. In the squares of the city, in the shadow of the steeple,
   Near the relief office, I see my people.
   And some are grumbling, and some are wondering
   If this land's still made for you and me.

WILDWOOD FLOWER

Traditional

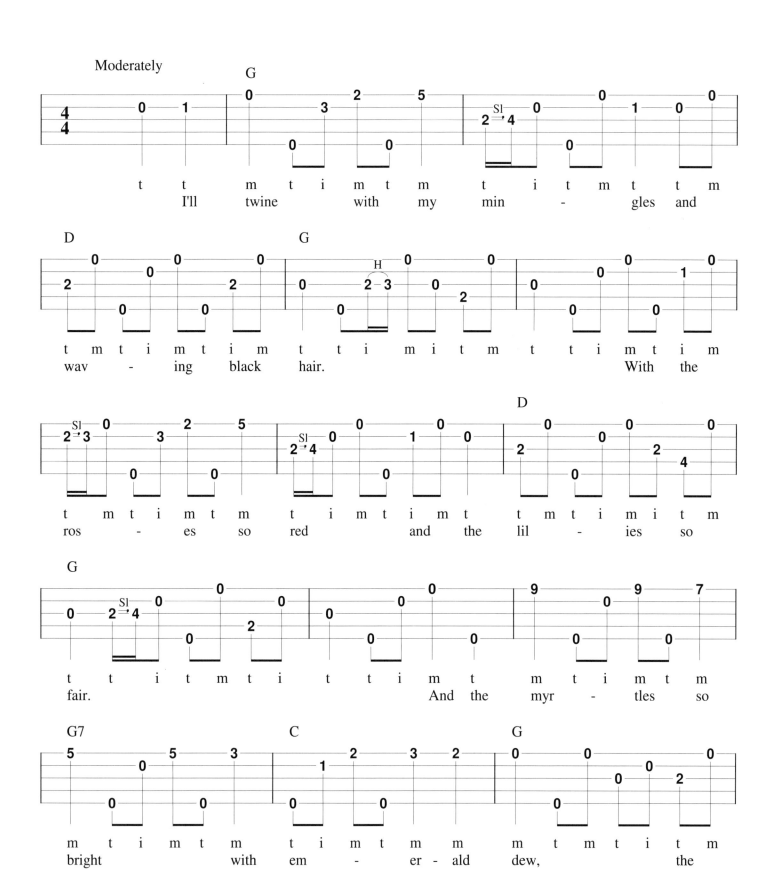

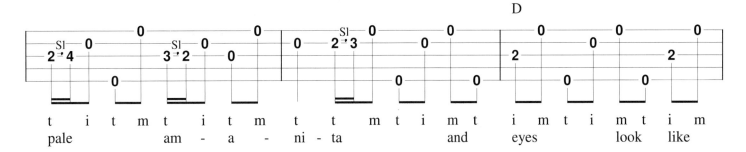

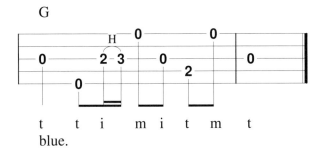

2. He told me he loved me and called me his flower
   That blossomed for him all the brighter each hour.
   Though my heart is now breaking, he never shall know
   That his name makes me tremble, my pale cheeks to glow.

3. I'll sing and I'll dance and my laugh shall be gay.
   I'll charm every heart and the crowd I will away.
   I'll live to see him regret the dark hour
   When he won and neglected this frail wildwood flower.

4. I'll think of him never, I'll be wild and gay.
   I'll cease this wild weeping, drive sorrow away.
   But I wake from my dreaming, my idol was clay;
   My visions of love have all vanished away.

WILL THE CIRCLE BE UNBROKEN

Words by Ada R. Habershon
Music by Charles H. Gabriel

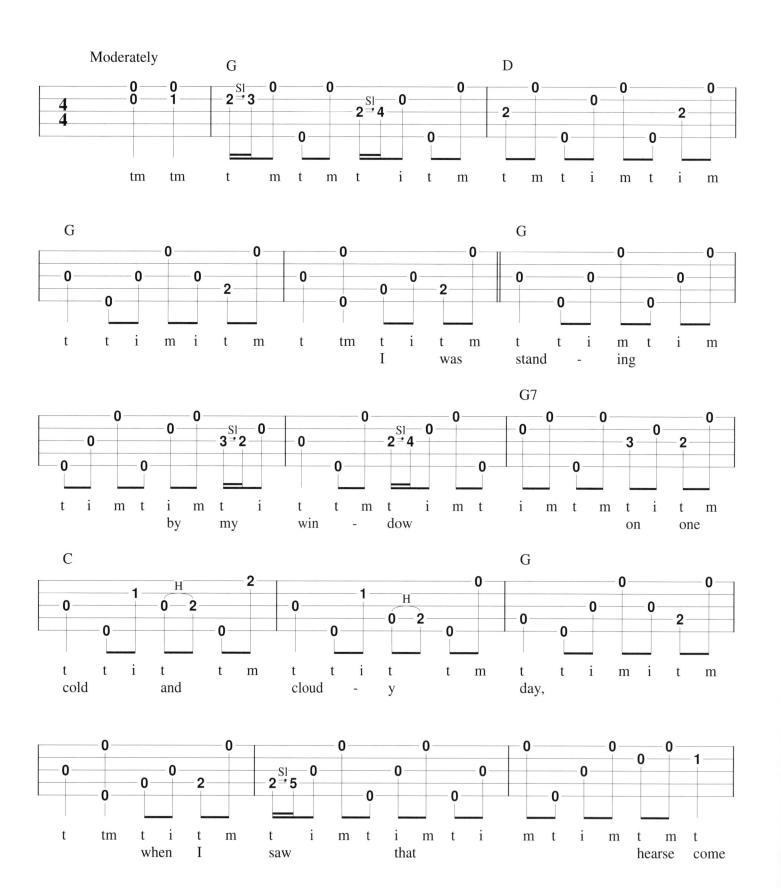

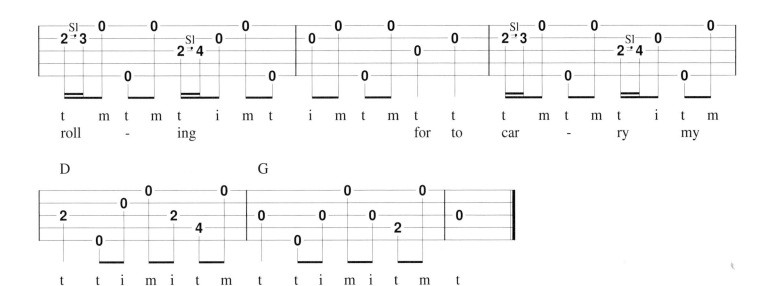

Chorus

Will the circle be unbroken, by and by, Lord, by and by?
There's a better home a-waiting, in the sky, Lord, in the sky.

2. I said to that undertaker, "Undertaker, please drive slow,
For this lady you are carrying, Lord, I hate to see her go".

Repeat Chorus

3. Oh, I followed close behind her, tried to hold up and be brave.
But I could not hide my sorrow when they laid her in the grave.

Repeat Chorus

4. I went back home, my home was lonesome, missed my mother, she was gone.
All my brothers, sisters crying, what a home so sad and alone.

Repeat Chorus

PUFF THE MAGIC DRAGON

Words and Music by
Lenny Lipton and Peter Yarrow

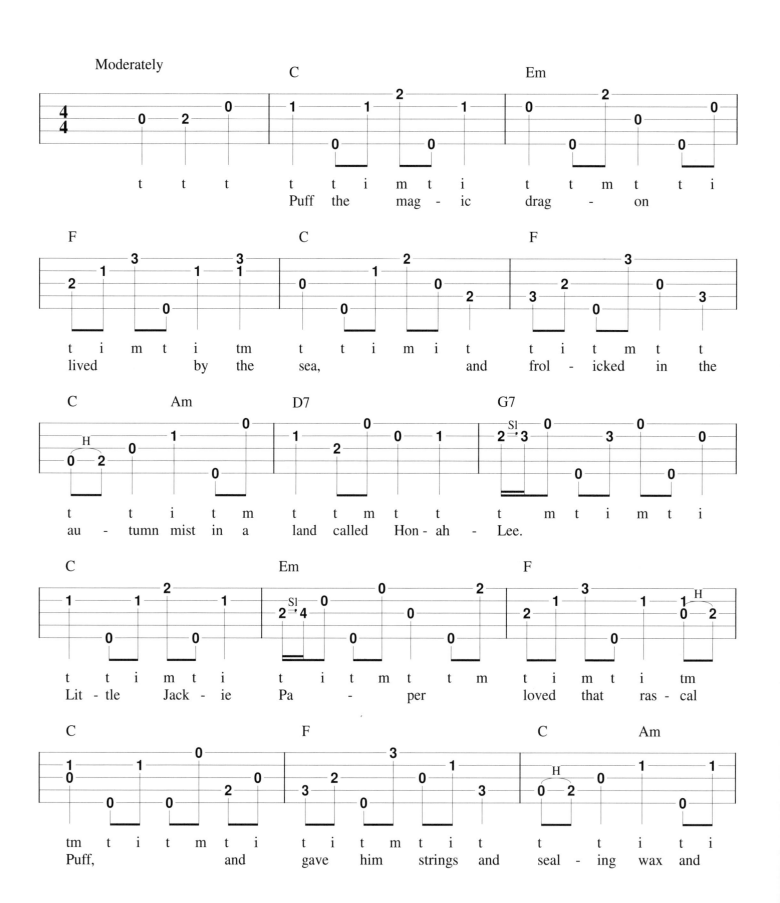

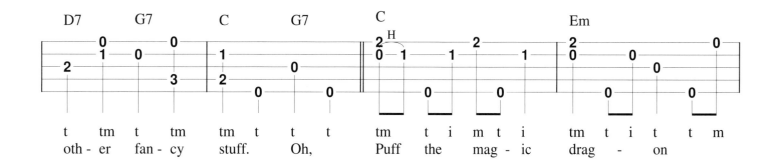

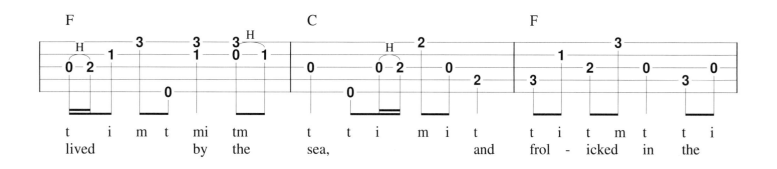

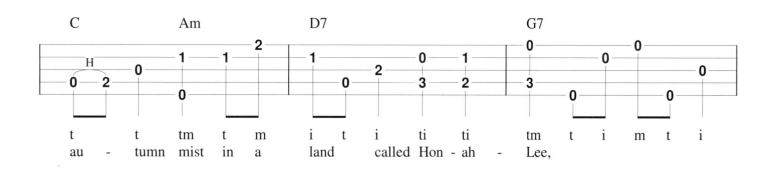

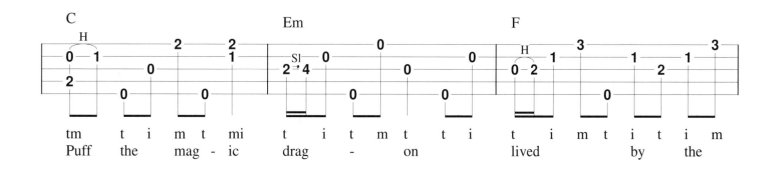

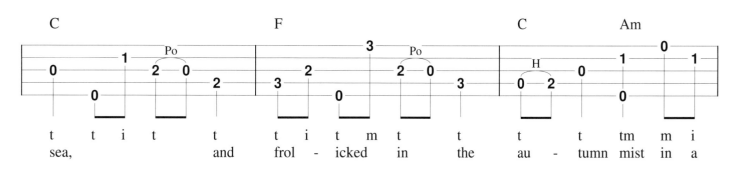

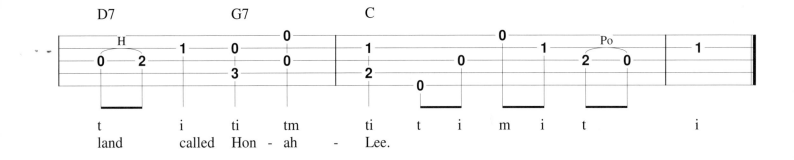

2. Together they would travel on a boat with billowed sail;
   Jackie kept a lookout perched on Puff's gigantic tail.
   Noble kings and princes would bow whenever they came;
   Pirate ships would lower their flags when Puff roared out his name. Oh!

   Chorus

   Puff, the magic dragon lived by the sea,
   And frolicked in the autumn mist in a land called Honah-Lee.
   Puff, the magic dragon lived by the sea,
   And frolicked in the autumn mist in a land called Honah-Lee.

3. A dragon lives forever but not so little boys;
   Painted wings and giants' rings make way for other toys.
   One grey night it happened, Jackie Paper came no more,
   And Puff that mighty dragon, he ceased his fearless roar.

4. His head was bent in sorrow, green scales fell like rain;
   Puff no longer went to play along the cherry lane.
   Without his lifelong friend, Puff could not be brave,
   So Puff that mighty dragon sadly slipped into his cave. Oh!

   Repeat Chorus